VEGETABLES
BEST-EVER VEGETABLE RECIPES

VEGETABLES
BEST-EVER VEGETABLE RECIPES

bay books

MEAL PLANNER

Use the following table to plan your best-ever Vegetable meal. The recipes have been grouped into appropriate classifications and the portion size of each recipe is clearly shown. Plan your meal and then turn to the appropriate page to find your clear and concise recipe together with a large-format picture of the finished dish.

SALADS, SNACKS & STARTERS

PIES & TARTS

INGREDIENTS

1 tablespoon olive oil
1 large onion, chopped
5 garlic cloves, chopped
1 large carrot, chopped
1 bay leaf
2 celery stalks, chopped
1 teaspoon ground cumin
$1/2$ teaspoon ground cinnamon
3 x 425 g (15 oz) cans chickpeas, drained and rinsed
1.25 litres (5 cups) chicken stock
1 tablespoon finely chopped flat-leaf (Italian) parsley, plus
    extra, to garnish
1 tablespoon finely chopped coriander (cilantro) leaves
2 tablespoons lemon juice
extra virgin olive oil, to drizzle

Spiced pitta bread
40 g ($1^1/2$ oz) butter
2 tablespoons olive oil
2 garlic cloves, crushed
$1/8$ teaspoon ground cumin
$1/8$ teaspoon ground cinnamon
$1/8$ teaspoon cayenne pepper
$1/2$ teaspoon sea salt
4 small pitta breads, split

1 Heat the oil in a large saucepan and cook the onion over medium heat for 3–4 minutes, or until soft. Add the garlic, carrot, bay leaf and celery and cook for 4 minutes, or until the vegetables start to caramelize.

2 Stir in the cumin and cinnamon and cook for 1 minute. Add the chickpeas, stock and 1 litre (4 cups) water and bring to the boil. Reduce the heat and simmer for 1 hour. Allow to cool.

3 Remove the bay leaf and purée the soup. Return to the cleaned pan and stir over medium heat until warmed. Stir in the herbs and lemon juice. Season. Drizzle with oil and garnish with parsley.

4 To make the spiced pitta bread, melt the butter and oil in a saucepan over medium heat. Add the garlic, spices and salt and cook for 1 minute. Place the pitta (smooth side up) on a lined tray and grill (broil) for 1–2 minutes, or until golden. Turn and brush with the spiced butter. Grill until golden and serve with the soup.

INGREDIENTS

2 tablespoons olive oil
1 small leek (white part only), chopped
2 garlic cloves, crushed
2 teaspoons curry powder
1 teaspoon ground cumin
1 teaspoon garam masala
1 litre (4 cups) vegetable stock
1 fresh bay leaf
185 g (1 cup) brown lentils
450 g (1 lb) butternut pumpkin (squash), peeled and cut into
    1 cm ($^1/_2$ inch) cubes
400 g (14 oz) can chopped tomatoes
2 zucchini (courgettes), cut in half lengthways and sliced
200 g (7 oz) broccoli, cut into small florets
1 small carrot, diced
80 g ($^1/_2$ cup) peas
1 tablespoon chopped mint

Spiced yoghurt
250 g (1 cup) thick natural yoghurt
1 tablespoon chopped coriander (cilantro) leaves
1 garlic clove, crushed
3 dashes Tabasco sauce

1   Heat the oil in a saucepan over medium heat. Add the leek and garlic and cook for
    4–5 minutes, or until soft and lightly golden. Add the curry powder, cumin and garam
    masala and cook for 1 minute, or until the spices are fragrant.

2   Add the stock, bay leaf, lentils and pumpkin. Bring to the boil, then reduce the heat to low
    and simmer for 10–15 minutes, or until the lentils are tender. Season well.

3   Add the tomatoes, zucchini, broccoli, carrot and 500 ml (2 cups) water and simmer for
    10 minutes, or until the vegetables are tender. Add the peas and simmer for 2–3 minutes.

4   To make the spiced yoghurt, place the yoghurt, coriander, garlic and Tabasco in a small
    bowl and stir until combined. Dollop a spoonful of the yoghurt on each serving of soup
    and garnish with the chopped mint.

ORANGE SWEET POTATO SOUP

40 g (1$^1/_2$ oz) butter
2 onions, chopped
2 garlic cloves, crushed
1 kg (2 lb 4 oz) orange sweet potato (kumera), peeled and chopped
1 large celery stalk, chopped
1 large green apple, peeled, cored and chopped
1$^1/_2$ teaspoons ground cumin
2 litres (8 cups) chicken stock
125 g ($^1/_2$ cup) thick natural yoghurt
lavash bread, to serve (optional)

1 Melt the butter in a large pan over low heat. Add the onion and cook, stirring occasionally, for 10 minutes, or until soft. Add the garlic, sweet potato, celery, apple and 1 teaspoon of the cumin and continue to cook for 5–7 minutes, or until well coated. Add the chicken stock and the remaining cumin and bring to the boil over high heat. Reduce the heat and simmer for 25–30 minutes, or until the sweet potato is very soft.

2 Cool the soup slightly and blend in batches until smooth. Return to the cleaned pan and gently stir over medium heat until warmed through. Season with salt and freshly ground black pepper. Divide among serving bowls and top each serve with a dollop of yoghurt.

3 Cut the lavash bread into rectangular strips, brush lightly with oil and place on a baking tray. Bake in a 190°C (375°F/Gas 5) oven for 15–20 minutes, or until crisp and lightly golden. Serve with the soup.

INGREDIENTS

40 g (1¹/₂ oz) butter
1 large onion, chopped
2 garlic cloves, crushed
500 g (1 lb 2 oz) carrots, sliced
125 ml (¹/₂ cup) orange juice
750 g (1 lb 10 oz) butternut pumpkin (squash), peeled and
   roughly chopped
1.5 litres (6 cups) chicken stock
1 tablespoon snipped chives
herb scones or herb bread, to serve

1   Melt the butter in a large saucepan over medium heat and cook the onion for 5 minutes, or until soft and starting to brown. Add the garlic and carrot and cook for another 5 minutes, or until starting to soften. Pour in the orange juice and bring to the boil over high heat. Add the pumpkin, stock and 500 ml (2 cups) water and return to the boil. Reduce the heat and simmer for 30 minutes, or until the carrot and pumpkin are soft.

2   Blend the soup in batches in a blender until smooth — add a little more stock if you prefer the soup to be a thinner consistency.

3   Return to the cleaned pan and reheat. Season to taste with salt and freshly ground pepper. Divide the soup among serving bowls and garnish with the chives. Serve with herb scones or bread.

PUMPKIN SOUP

2 kg (4 lb 8 oz) butternut pumpkin (squash)
40 g (1¹/₂ oz) butter
2 onions, chopped
¹/₂ teaspoon cumin seeds
1 litre (4 cups) chicken stock
1 bay leaf
80 ml (¹/₃ cup) cream
pinch nutmeg

1 Peel the pumpkin and chop into small chunks. Melt the butter in a large saucepan, add the onion and cook over low heat for 5–7 minutes, or until soft. Add the cumin seeds and cook for 1 minute, then add the pumpkin pieces, stock and bay leaf. Increase the heat to high and bring to the boil, then reduce the heat and simmer for 20 minutes, or until the pumpkin is soft. Remove the bay leaf and allow the soup to cool slightly.

2 Blend the soup in batches until it is smooth. Return to the cleaned pan and stir in the cream and nutmeg. Simmer gently until warmed through and season with salt and freshly ground black pepper before serving.

2 tablespoons olive oil

1 large red onion, finely chopped

2 garlic cloves, crushed

2 tablespoons tomato paste (purée)

2 tomatoes, finely chopped

2 teaspoons paprika

1 teaspoon cayenne pepper

500 g (2 cups) red lentils

50 g (¼ cup) long-grain rice

2.125 litres (8½ cups) chicken stock

45 g (¼ cup) fine burghul (bulgar wheat)

2 tablespoons chopped mint

2 tablespoons chopped flat-leaf (Italian) parsley

90 g (⅓ cup) thick natural yoghurt

¼ preserved lemon, pulp removed, zest washed and julienned

1 Heat the oil in a saucepan over medium heat. Add the onion and garlic and cook for 2–3 minutes, or until soft. Stir in the tomato paste, tomato and spices and cook for 1 minute.

2 Add the lentils, rice and chicken stock, then cover and bring to the boil over high heat. Reduce the heat and simmer for 30–35 minutes, or until the rice is cooked.

3 Stir in the burghul and herbs, then season to taste. Divide the soup among serving bowls, garnish with yoghurt and preserved lemon and serve immediately.

NOTE This soup will thicken on standing, so if reheating you may need to add more liquid.

RED LENTIL, BURGHUL AND MINT SOUP

INGREDIENTS

200 g (6½ oz) pearl barley
1 tablespoon oil
2 onions, chopped
2 cloves garlic, finely chopped
2 carrots, chopped
2 potatoes, chopped
2 celery sticks, chopped
2 bay leaves, torn in half
2 litres chicken stock
½ cup (125 ml/4 fl oz) milk
40 g (1¼ oz) butter
3 parsnips, cubed
1 teaspoon soft brown sugar
chopped fresh parsley, to serve

1   Soak the barley in water overnight. Drain. Place in a saucepan with 2 litres water. Bring to the boil, then reduce the heat and simmer, partially covered, for 1¼ hours, or until tender. Drain the barley.

2   Heat the oil in a large saucepan, add the onion, garlic, carrot, potato and celery, and cook for 3 minutes. Stir well and cook, covered, for 15 minutes over low heat, stirring occasionally.

3   Add the barley, bay leaves, stock, milk, 2 teaspoons of salt and 1 teaspoon of pepper. Bring to the boil, then reduce the heat and simmer the soup, partially covered, for 35 minutes. If the soup is too thick, add about 1 cup (250 ml/8 fl oz) cold water, a little at a time, until the soup reaches your preferred consistency.

4   While the soup is simmering, melt the butter in a frying pan, add the parsnip and toss in the butter. Sprinkle with the sugar and cook until golden brown and tender. Serve the parsnip on top of the soup and sprinkle with the parsley.

INGREDIENTS

1 tablespoon oil
1 onion, chopped
2 cloves garlic, crushed
2 teaspoons ground cumin
1 teaspoon ground coriander (cilantro)
¼ teaspoon chilli powder
2 x 300 g (10 oz) cans chickpeas, drained
3½ cups (875 ml/28 fl oz) vegetable stock
2 x 425 g (14 oz) cans chopped tomatoes
1 tablespoon chopped fresh coriander (cilantro) leaves
1 cup (125 g/4 oz) self-raising flour
25 g (¾ oz) butter, chopped
2 tablespoons grated fresh Parmesan
2 tablespoons mixed chopped fresh herbs (chives, flat-leaf parsley and coriander leaves)
¼ cup (60 ml/2 fl oz) milk

1   Heat the oil in a large saucepan and cook the onion over medium heat for 2–3 minutes, or until soft. Add the garlic, cumin, ground coriander and chilli, and cook for 1 minute, or until fragrant. Add the chickpeas, stock and tomato. Bring to the boil, then reduce the heat and simmer, covered, for 10 minutes. Stir in the coriander.

2   To make the dumplings, sift the flour into a bowl and add the chopped butter. Rub the butter into the flour with your fingertips until it resembles fine breadcrumbs. Stir in the cheese and mixed fresh herbs. Make a well in the centre, add the milk and mix with a flat-bladed knife until just combined. Bring the dough together into a rough ball, divide into eight portions and roll into small balls.

3   Add the dumplings to the soup, cover and simmer for 20 minutes, or until a skewer comes out clean when inserted into the centre of the dumplings.

INGREDIENTS

1/2 cup (100 g/31/2 oz) dried red kidney beans or borlotti beans
1 tablespoon olive oil
1 leek, halved lengthways, chopped
1 small onion, diced
2 carrots, chopped
2 celery sticks, chopped
1 large zucchini (courgette), chopped
1 tablespoon tomato paste (purée)
1 litre (4 cups) vegetable stock
400 g (13 oz) pumpkin, cut into 2 cm (3/4 inch) cubes
2 potatoes, cut into 2 cm (3/4 inch) cubes
1/4 cup (7 g/1/4 oz) chopped fresh flat-leaf parsley

1 Put the beans in a large bowl, cover with cold water and soak overnight. Rinse, then transfer to a saucepan, cover with cold water and cook for 45 minutes, or until just tender. Drain.

2 Meanwhile, heat the oil in a large saucepan. Add the leek and onion, and cook over medium heat for 2–3 minutes without browning, or until they start to soften. Add the carrot, celery and zucchini, and cook for 3–4 minutes. Add the tomato paste and stir for a further 1 minute. Pour in the stock and 1.25 litres water, and bring to the boil. Reduce the heat to low and simmer for 20 minutes.

3 Add the pumpkin, potato, parsley and red kidney beans, and simmer for a further 20 minutes, or until the vegetables are tender and the beans are cooked. Season to taste. Serve immediately with crusty wholemeal or wholegrain bread.

INGREDIENTS

6 large potatoes, unpeeled
oil, for deep-frying

1 Preheat the oven to hot 210°C (415°F/Gas 6–7). Prick each potato with a fork and bake for 1 hour, or until the skins are crisp and the flesh is soft. Turn once during cooking.

2 Leave the potatoes to cool, then halve them and scoop out the flesh, leaving a thin layer of potato in each shell. Cut each half into 3 wedges.

3 Fill a deep heavy-based pan one-third full of oil and heat to 190°C (375°F). or until a cube of bread browns in 10 seconds. Cook the potato skins in batches for 2–3 minutes, or until crisp. Drain on paper towels. Sprinkle with salt and pepper.

INGREDIENTS

500 g (1 lb) orange sweet potato (kumera), peeled and cut into chunks
1 red or yellow capsicum (pepper), cut into chunks
2 zucchini (courgette), sliced
350 g (12 oz) eggplant (aubergine), cut into chunks
2 tomatoes, cut into chunks
8 spring onions, cut into lengths
1 tablespoon extra virgin olive oil
1 teaspoon sea salt
1 teaspoon grated lemon zest
2 tablespoons lemon juice

1   Preheat the oven to hot 220°C (425°F/Gas 7). Place the vegetables in a large baking
    dish, drizzle with oil, sprinkle with sea salt and roast for 45 minutes, or until soft.

2   Transfer the vegetables to a food processor, add the lemon zest and the lemon juice.
    Blend until smooth. Spoon into a serving dish and cool to room temperature.

INGREDIENTS

2 corn cobs
3 tablespoons chopped fresh coriander (cilantro) leaves
6 spring onions, finely chopped
1 small red chilli, seeded and finely chopped
1 large egg
2 teaspoons ground cumin
$1/2$ teaspoon ground coriander (cilantro)
1 cup (125 g) plain flour
oil, for deep-frying
sweet chilli sauce, to serve

1   Cut down the side of the corn with a sharp knife to release the kernels. Roughly chop the kernels, then place them in a large bowl. Holding the cobs over the bowl, scrape down the sides of the cobs with a knife to release any corn juice from the cob into the bowl.

2   Add the fresh coriander, spring onion, chilli, egg, cumin, ground coriander, 1 teaspoon salt and some cracked black pepper to the bowl and stir well. Add the flour and mix well. The texture of the batter will vary depending on the juiciness of the corn. If the mixture is too dry, add 1 tablespoon water, but no more than that as the batter should be quite dry. Stand for 10 minutes.

3   Fill a large heavy-based saucepan or deep-fryer one-third full of oil and heat to 180°C (350°F), or until a cube of bread dropped in the oil browns in 15 seconds. Drop slightly heaped teaspoons of the corn batter into the oil and cook for about $1^{1}/_{2}$ minutes, or until puffed and golden. Drain on crumpled paper towels and serve immediately with a bowl of the sweet chilli sauce to dip the puffs into.

INGREDIENTS

400 g English spinach
30 g (1 oz) butter
$1/2$ teaspoon ground coriander (cilantro)
pinch cayenne pepper
2 spring onions, roughly chopped
1 clove garlic
$1/3$ cup (50 g/$1^3/_4$ oz) blanched almonds
2 teaspoons white wine vinegar
$1/2$ cup (125 g/$4^1/_2$ oz) sour cream

1   Remove the stems from the spinach. Wash the leaves and place wet in a pan. Cover and cook for 2 minutes, or until wilted, then drain, reserving $1/4$ cup (60 ml) of the cooking liquid. Cool the spinach then squeeze dry.

2   Melt the butter in a small pan. Add the coriander, cayenne pepper, spring onion, garlic and almonds, and cook until the onion is tender. Cool.

3   Place in a food processor and process until finely chopped. Add the spinach and process, gradually adding the reserved cooking liquid and vinegar.

4   Stir in the sour cream and season well with salt and pepper.

2 kg (4 lb) round ricotta cheese

olive oil

2 cloves garlic, crushed

1 preserved lemon, rinsed, pith and flesh removed, cut into thin strips

150 g (5 oz) semi-dried (sun-blushed) tomatoes, roughly chopped

1 cup (30 g/1 oz) finely chopped fresh flat-leaf parsley

1 cup (50 g/1³/₄ oz) chopped fresh coriander (cilantro) leaves

¹/₃ cup (80 ml/2³/₄ fl oz) extra virgin olive oil

3 tablespoons lemon juice

1   Preheat the oven to very hot 250°C (500°F/Gas 10). Place the ricotta on a baking tray lined with baking paper, brush lightly with the olive oil and bake for 20–30 minutes, or until golden brown. Leave for 10 minutes then, using egg flips, transfer to a large platter. (If possible, have someone help you move the ricotta.)

2   Meanwhile, place the garlic, preserved lemon, semi-dried tomato, parsley, coriander, oil and lemon juice in a bowl and mix together well.

3   Spoon the dressing over the baked ricotta and serve with crusty bread. It is delicious hot or cold.

BAKED RICOTTA WITH PRESERVED LEMON AND SEMI-DRIED TOMATOES

INGREDIENTS

60 g (2 oz) butter
2 leeks, sliced
2 cloves garlic, crushed
1 kg (2 lb) carrots, sliced
1½ cups (375 ml/12 fl oz) vegetable stock
1½ tablespoons finely chopped fresh sage
¼ cup (60 ml/2 fl oz) cream
4 eggs, lightly beaten

Creamy saffron and leek sauce
40 g (1¼ oz) butter
1 small leek, finely sliced
1 large clove garlic, crushed
¼ cup (60 ml/2 fl oz) white wine
pinch of saffron threads
⅓ cup (90 g/3 oz) crème fraîche

1   Preheat the oven to warm 170°C (325°F/Gas 3). Lightly grease six ¾ cup (185 ml) timbale moulds. Heat the butter in a saucepan and cook the leek for 3–4 minutes, or until soft. Add the garlic and carrot and cook for a further 2–3 minutes. Pour in the stock and 2 cups (500 ml/16 fl oz) water, bring to the boil, then reduce the heat and simmer, covered, for 5 minutes, or until the carrot is tender. Strain, reserving ³/₄ cup (185 ml/6 fl oz) of the liquid.

2   Blend the carrot mixture, ½ cup (125 ml/4 fl oz) of the reserved liquid and the sage in a food processor or blender until smooth. Cool the mixture slightly and stir in the cream and egg. Season and pour into the prepared moulds. Place the moulds in a roasting tin filled with enough hot water to come halfway up their sides. Bake for 30–40 minutes, or until just set.

3   To make the sauce, melt the butter in a saucepan and cook the leek for 3–4 minutes without browning. Add the garlic and cook for 30 seconds. Add the wine, remaining reserved liquid and saffron and bring to the boil. Reduce the heat and simmer for 5 minutes, or until reduced. Stir in the crème fraîche.

4   Turn out the timbales onto serving plates and serve with the sauce.

INGREDIENTS

Tomato salsa

2 ripe tomatoes

1 cup (150 g/5 oz) frozen broad beans

2 tablespoons chopped fresh basil

1 small Lebanese cucumber, diced

2 small cloves garlic, crushed

1¹/₂ tablespoons balsamic vinegar

1 tablespoon extra virgin olive oil

Corn and polenta pancakes

³/₄ cup (90 g/3 oz) self-raising flour

³/₄ cup (110 g/3¹/₂ oz) fine polenta

1 cup (250 ml/8 fl oz) milk

310 g (10 oz) can corn kernels

olive oil, for frying

1 To make the salsa, score a cross in the base of each tomato, then place in a bowl of boiling water for 30 seconds. Plunge into cold water and peel the skin away from the cross. Dice. Pour boiling water over the broad beans and leave for 2–3 minutes. Drain and rinse under cold water. Remove the skins. Put the beans in a bowl and stir in the tomato, basil, cucumber, garlic, vinegar and extra virgin olive oil.

2 To make the pancakes, sift the flour into a bowl and stir in the polenta. Add the milk and corn and stir until just combined, adding more milk if the batter is too dry. Season.

3 Heat the oil in a large frying pan and spoon half the batter into the pan, making four 9 cm (3¹/₂ inch) pancakes. Cook for 2 minutes each side, or until golden and cooked through. Repeat with the remaining batter, adding more oil if necessary. Drain well and serve with the salsa.

FRIED TOMATOES WITH MARINATED HALOUMI

400 g (13 oz) haloumi cheese, cut into eight 1 cm ($^1/_2$ inch) slices
250 g (8 oz) cherry tomatoes, halved
250 g (8 oz) teardrop tomatoes, halved
1 clove garlic, crushed
2 tablespoons lemon juice
1 tablespoon balsamic vinegar
2 teaspoons fresh lemon thyme
$^1/_4$ cup (60 ml) extra virgin olive oil
2 tablespoons olive oil
1 small loaf wholegrain bread, cut into 8 thick slices

1 Place the haloumi and tomatoes in a non-metallic dish. Whisk together the garlic, lemon juice, balsamic vinegar, thyme and extra virgin olive oil in a jug and pour over the haloumi and tomatoes. Cover and marinate for 3 hours or overnight. Drain well, reserving the marinade.

2 Heat the olive oil in a large frying pan. Add the haloumi and cook in batches over medium heat for 1 minute each side, or until golden brown. Transfer to a plate and keep warm. Add the tomatoes and cook over medium heat for 5 minutes, or until their skins begin to burst. Transfer to a plate and keep warm.

3 Toast the bread until it is golden brown. Serve the fried haloumi on top of the toasted bread, piled high with the tomatoes and drizzled with the reserved marinade. Best served immediately.

INGREDIENTS

½ cup (125 ml/4 fl oz) oil
2 zucchini (courgettes), sliced on the diagonal
500 g (1 lb) eggplant (aubergine), sliced
1 small fennel bulb, sliced
1 red onion, sliced
300 g (10 oz) ricotta cheese
60 g (2 oz) Parmesan, grated
1 tablespoon chopped fresh flat-leaf parsley
1 tablespoon chopped fresh chives
1 red capsicum (pepper), grilled, peeled and cut into large
   pieces
1 yellow capsicum (pepper), grilled, peeled and cut into
   large pieces

Spicy tomato sauce

1 tablespoon oil
1 onion, finely chopped
2 cloves garlic, crushed
1 red chilli, seeded and chopped
425 g (14 oz) can chopped tomatoes
2 tablespoons tomato paste (purée)

1   Heat 1 tablespoon of the oil in a large frying pan. Cook the vegetables in separate batches over high heat for 5 minutes, or until golden, adding the remaining oil as needed. Drain each vegetable separately on paper towels.

2   Preheat the oven to moderately hot 200°C (400°F/Gas 6). Place the cheeses and herbs in a small bowl and mix together well. Season to taste.

3   Lightly grease four 1¼ cup (315 ml/10 fl oz) ramekins and line with baking paper. Using half the eggplant, put a layer in the base of each dish. Layer the zucchini, capsicum, cheese mixture, fennel and onion over the eggplant. Cover with the remaining eggplant and press down firmly. Bake for 10–15 minutes, or until hot. Leave for 5 minutes before turning out.

4   To make the sauce, heat the oil in a saucepan and cook the onion and garlic for 2–3 minutes, or until soft. Add the chilli, tomato and tomato paste and simmer for 5 minutes, or until thick and pulpy. Purée in a food processor. Return to the saucepan and keep warm. Spoon over the terrines.

INGREDIENTS

2 eggplants (aubergine)
1 tablespoon oil
1 onion, finely chopped
2 cloves garlic, crushed
2 ripe tomatoes, peeled, seeded and chopped
2 teaspoons tomato paste (purée)
½ teaspoon dried oregano
½ cup (125 ml/4 fl oz) dry white wine
300 g (10 oz) can soya beans, rinsed and drained
3 tablespoons chopped fresh flat-leaf parsley
30 g (1 oz) butter
2 tablespoons plain (all-purpose) flour
pinch of ground nutmeg
1¼ cups (315 ml/10 fl oz) milk
⅓ cup (40 g/1¼ oz) grated Cheddar

1 Preheat the oven to moderate 180°C (350°F/Gas 4). Cut the eggplants in half lengthways. Spoon out the flesh, leaving a narrow border and place on a large baking tray, cut-side-up. Use crumpled foil around the sides of the eggplant to help support it.

2 Heat the oil in a large frying pan. Cook the onion and garlic over medium heat for 3 minutes, or until soft. Add the tomato, tomato paste, oregano and wine. Boil for 3 minutes, or until the liquid is reduced and the tomato is soft. Stir in the soya beans and parsley.

3 To make the sauce, melt the butter in a saucepan. Stir in the flour and cook over medium heat for 1 minute, or until pale and foamy. Remove from the heat and gradually stir in the nutmeg and milk. Return to the heat and stir constantly until the sauce boils and thickens. Pour one third of the white sauce into the tomato mixture and stir well.

4 Spoon the mixture into the eggplant shells. Smooth the surface before spreading the remaining sauce evenly over the top and sprinkling with cheese. Bake for 50 minutes, or until cooked through. Serve hot.

INGREDIENTS

Hollandaise sauce
175 g (6 oz) butter
4 egg yolks
1 tablespoon lemon juice

4 eggs, at room temperature
310 g (10 oz) asparagus spears, trimmed
Parmesan shavings, to serve

1   To make the hollandaise, melt the butter in a small saucepan and skim off any froth. Remove from the heat and cool. Mix the egg yolks and 2 tablespoons water in another small saucepan for 30 seconds, or until pale and foamy. Place the saucepan over very low heat and whisk for 2–3 minutes, or until thick and foamy—do not overheat or it will scramble. Remove from the heat. Gradually add the butter, whisking well after each addition (avoid using the whey at the bottom). Stir in the lemon juice and season. If the sauce is runny, return to the heat and whisk until thick—do not scramble.

2   Place the eggs in a saucepan half filled with water. Bring to the boil and cook for 6–7 minutes, stirring occasionally to centre the yolks. Drain and cover with cold water until cooled a little, then peel off the shells.

3   Plunge the asparagus into a large saucepan of boiling water and cook for 3 minutes, or until just tender. Drain and pat dry. Divide among four plates. Spoon on the hollandaise. Cut the eggs in half and arrange two halves on each plate. Sprinkle with Parmesan shavings to serve.

ASPARAGUS AND MUSHROOM SALAD

155 g (5 oz) asparagus spears
1 tablespoon wholegrain mustard
¼ cup (60 ml/2 fl oz) orange juice
2 tablespoons lemon juice
1 tablespoon lime juice
1 tablespoon orange zest
2 teaspoons lemon zest
2 teaspoons lime zest
2 cloves garlic, crushed
¼ cup (90 g/3 oz) honey
400 g (13 oz) button mushrooms, halved
150 g (5 oz) rocket
1 red capsicum (pepper), cut into strips

1 Snap the woody ends from the asparagus spears and cut in half on the diagonal. Cook in boiling water for 1 minute, or until just tender. Drain, plunge into cold water and set aside.

2 Place the mustard, citrus juice and zest, garlic and honey in a large saucepan and season with pepper. Bring to the boil, then reduce the heat and add the mushrooms, tossing for 2 minutes. Cool.

3 Remove the mushrooms from the sauce with a slotted spoon. Return the sauce to the heat, bring to the boil, then reduce the heat and simmer for 3–5 minutes, or until reduced and syrupy. Cool slightly.

4 Toss the mushrooms, rocket leaves, capsicum and asparagus. Put on a plate and drizzle with the sauce.

INGREDIENTS

500 g (1 lb) butternut pumpkin (squash), cubed

2 red capsicums (peppers), halved

4 slender eggplants (aubergines), cut in half lengthways

4 zucchini (courgettes), cut in half lengthways

4 onions, quartered

olive oil, for brushing

2 x 300 g (10 oz) cans chickpeas, rinsed and drained

2 tablespoons chopped fresh flat-leaf parsley

Dressing

⅓ cup (80 ml/2¾ fl oz) olive oil

2 tablespoons lemon juice

1 clove garlic, crushed

1 tablespoon chopped fresh thyme

1 Preheat the oven to hot 220°C (425°F/Gas 7). Brush two baking trays with oil and lay out the vegetables in a single layer. Brush lightly with oil.

2 Bake for 40 minutes, or until the vegetables are tender and begin to brown slightly on the edges. Cool. Remove the skins from the capsicum if you want. Chop the capsicum, eggplant and zucchini into pieces, then put the vegetables in a bowl with the chickpeas and half the parsley.

3 Whisk together all the dressing ingredients. Season, then toss with the vegetables. Leave for 30 minutes, then sprinkle with the rest of the parsley.

INGREDIENTS

1 kg (2 lb) (4 bulbs with leaves) fresh beetroot
200 g (6½ oz) green beans
1 tablespoon red wine vinegar
2 tablespoons extra virgin olive oil
1 clove garlic, crushed
1 tablespoon drained capers, coarsely chopped
100 g (31/2 oz) goat's cheese

1 Trim the leaves from the beetroot. Scrub the bulbs and wash the leaves well. Add the whole bulbs to a large saucepan of boiling water, reduce the heat and simmer, covered, for 30 minutes, or until tender when pierced with the point of a knife. (The cooking time may vary depending on the size of the bulbs.)

2 Meanwhile, bring a saucepan of water to the boil, add the beans and cook for 3 minutes, or until just tender. Remove with a slotted spoon and plunge into a bowl of cold water. Drain well. Add the beetroot leaves to the same saucepan of boiling water and cook for 3–5 minutes, or until the leaves and stems are tender. Drain, plunge into a bowl of cold water, then drain again well.

3 Drain and cool the beetroots, then peel the skins off and cut the bulbs into thin wedges.

4 To make the dressing, put the red wine vinegar, oil, garlic, capers, ½ teaspoon salt and ½ teaspoon pepper in a screw-top jar and shake.

5 To serve, divide the beans, beetroot leaves and bulbs among four serving plates. Crumble goat's cheese over the top and drizzle with the dressing.

INGREDIENTS

6 tomatoes, cut into thin wedges
1 red onion, cut into thin rings
2 Lebanese cucumbers, sliced
1 cup (185 g/6 oz) Kalamata olives
200 g (6½ oz) feta cheese
1/2 cup (125 ml/4 fl oz) extra virgin olive oil
dried oregano, to sprinkle

1 Combine the tomato wedges with the onion rings, sliced cucumber and Kalamata olives in a large bowl. Season to taste with salt and freshly ground black pepper.

2 Break up the feta into large pieces with your fingers and scatter over the top of the salad. Drizzle with the olive oil and sprinkle with some oregano.

INGREDIENTS

900 g (1¾ lb) Hokkien noodles
6 spring onions, sliced diagonally
1 large red capsicum (pepper), thinly sliced
200 g (6½ oz) snow peas (mangetout), sliced
1 carrot, sliced diagonally
60 g (2 oz) fresh mint, chopped
60 g (2 oz) fresh coriander (cilantro), chopped
100 g (3½ oz) roasted cashew nuts

Sesame Dressing

2 teaspoons sesame oil
1 tablespoon peanut oil
2 tablespoons lime juice
2 tablespoons kecap manis (see note)
3 tablespoons sweet chilli sauce

1 Gently separate the noodles and place in a large bowl, cover with boiling water and leave for 2 minutes. Rinse and drain.

2 Put the noodles in a large bowl, and add spring onions, capsicum, snow peas, carrot, mint and coriander. Toss together well.

3 To make the dressing, whisk together the oils, lime juice, kecap manis and sweet chilli sauce. Pour the dressing over the salad and toss again. Sprinkle the cashew nuts over the top and serve immediately.

NOTE If you can't find kecap manis, you can use soy sauce sweetened with a little soft brown sugar.

INGREDIENTS

500 g (1 lb) new potatoes, unpeeled, halved

6 parsnips, peeled and quartered lengthways

500 g (1 lb) orange sweet potato (kumera), cut into large
pieces

335 g (11 oz) baby carrots, with stalks

6 pickling onions, halved

⅓ cup (80 ml/2¾ fl oz) oil

2 tablespoons poppy seeds

200 g (6½ oz) Brie cheese, thinly sliced

Orange Dressing

½ cup (125 ml/4 fl oz) orange juice

2 cloves garlic, crushed

1 tablespoon Dijon mustard

1 teaspoon white wine vinegar

1 teaspoon sesame oil

1 Preheat the oven to moderately hot 200°C (400°F/Gas 6). Place all the vegetables and the oil in a large deep baking dish. Toss the vegetables to coat with the oil. Bake for 50 minutes, or until the vegetables are crisp and tender, tossing every 15 minutes. Sprinkle with the poppy seeds.

2 Whisk together all the dressing ingredients.

3 Pour the dressing over the warm vegetables and toss to coat. Transfer to a large bowl, top with the Brie and serve immediately, while still warm.

ORANGE POPPY SEED ROASTED VEGETABLES

INGREDIENTS

200 g (6½ oz) haloumi cheese
¼ cup (60 ml/2 fl oz) olive oil
2 cloves garlic, crushed
1 tablespoon chopped fresh oregano
1 tablespoon chopped fresh marjoram
8 egg (Roma) tomatoes, halved
1 small red onion, cut into 8 wedges with base intact
¼ cup (60 ml/2 fl oz) olive oil, extra
2 tablespoons balsamic vinegar
150 g (5 oz) baby English spinach leaves

1   Cut the haloumi into 1 cm (½ inch) slices lengthways and put in a shallow dish.
    Mix together the oil, garlic and herbs and pour over the haloumi. Marinate, covered,
    for 1–2 hours.

2   Preheat the oven to moderately hot 200°C (400°F/Gas 6). Place the tomato and onion
    in a single layer in a roasting tin, drizzle with 2 tablespoons of the extra olive oil and
    1 tablespoon of the vinegar and sprinkle with salt and cracked black pepper. Bake for
    50–60 minutes, or until golden.

3   Meanwhile, heat a non-stick frying pan over medium heat. Drain the haloumi and cook for
    1 minute each side, or until golden brown.

4   Divide the spinach leaves among four serving plates and top with the tomato and onion.
    Whisk together the remaining olive oil and balsamic vinegar in a small bowl and drizzle
    over the salad. Top with the haloumi.

2 teaspoons yellow mustard seeds
2 teaspoons black mustard seeds
1 teaspoon ground turmeric
1 teaspoon tamarind purée
2–3 tablespoons mustard oil or oil
2 garlic cloves, finely chopped
$1/2$ onion, finely chopped
600 g (1 lb 5 oz) cauliflower, broken into small florets
3 mild green chillies, seeded and finely chopped
2 teaspoons kalonji (nigella) seeds

1 Grind the yellow and black mustard seeds together to a fine powder in a spice grinder or mortar and pestle. Mix with the turmeric, tamarind purée and 100 ml ($3^{1}/_{2}$ fl oz) water to form a smooth, quite liquid paste.

2 Heat 2 tablespoons of the oil in a large heavy-based saucepan over medium heat until almost smoking. Reduce the heat to low, add the garlic and onion and fry until golden. Cook the cauliflower in batches, adding more oil if necessary, and fry until lightly browned, then remove. Add the chilli and fry for 1 minute, or until tinged with brown around the edges.

3 Return all the cauliflower to the pan, sprinkle it with the mustard mixture and kalonji and stir well. Increase the heat to medium and bring to the boil, even though there's not much sauce. Reduce the heat to low, cover and cook until the cauliflower is nearly tender and the seasoning is dry. Sprinkle a little water on the cauliflower as it cooks to stop it sticking to the pan. If there is still excess liquid when the cauliflower is cooked, simmer with the lid off until it dries out. Season with salt, and remove from the heat. Serve with rice or Indian bread, or as an accompaniment to meat dishes.

CAULIFLOWER WITH MUSTARD

INGREDIENTS

1 teaspoon salt
2 cloves garlic, crushed
1 cup (150 g/5 oz) instant polenta
$1/2$ cup (125 ml/4 fl oz) cream
40 g ($1^1/_4$ oz) butter, chopped
$1/3$ cup (35 g/$1^1/_4$ oz) grated fresh Parmesan
$1/4$ teaspoon paprika, and extra to garnish
Parmesan shavings, to garnish

1 Bring $3^1/_2$ cups (875 ml/28 fl oz) water to the boil in a large, heavy-based saucepan.
Add the salt and crushed garlic. Stir in the polentawith a wooden spoon, breaking up any
lumps. Cook over medium heat for 4–5 minutes, or until smooth, stirring often.

2 Add half the cream and cook for 2–3 minutes, or until the polenta is thick and comes
away from the pan. Stir in the butter. Remove from the heat and stir in the Parmesan,
paprika and remaining cream. Transfer to a warm serving bowl and sprinkle with paprika.
Garnish with Parmesan shavings and serve at once.

NOTE Polenta must be served hot to keep its creamy, light consistency.

INGREDIENTS

2 large (600 g/1 lb 5 oz) eggplants (aubergines)
1 red onion, chopped
1 garlic clove, chopped
2.5 cm (1 inch) piece of ginger, chopped
1 green chilli, chopped
100 ml (3^1/$_2$ fl oz) oil
^{1}/$_4$ teaspoon chilli powder
^{1}/$_2$ teaspoon garam masala
2 teaspoons ground cumin
2 teaspoons ground coriander (cilantro)
2 teaspoons salt
^{1}/$_2$ teaspoon ground black pepper
2 ripe tomatoes, chopped
3–4 tablespoons coriander (cilantro) leaves, finely chopped

1   Using a pair of tongs, scorch the eggplants by holding them over a medium gas flame. Alternatively, heat them under a grill (broiler) or on an electric hotplate. Keep turning them until the skin is blackened on all sides. Set aside until cool, then peel off the charred skin. Roughly chop the flesh. Don't worry if black specks remain on the flesh because they add to the smoky flavour.

2   Combine the onion, garlic, ginger and chilli in a blender and process until chopped together but not a paste. Alternatively, chop finely with a knife and mix in a bowl.

3   Heat the oil in a deep heavy-based frying pan over medium heat, add the onion mixture and cook until slightly browned. Add all the spices and the salt and pepper and stir for 1 minute. Add the tomato and simmer until the liquid has reduced.

4   Put the eggplants in the pan and mash them with a wooden spoon, stirring around with the spices. Simmer for 10 minutes, or until soft. Stir in the coriander leaves and season with salt. Serve with bread as a light meal, or as a cold relish with a main meal, such as an Indian curry.

SPANISH CRISP POTATOES IN SPICY TOMATO SAUCE

olive oil, for deep-frying

1 kg (2 lb 4 oz) desiree potatoes, peeled and cut into 2 cm (³/₄ inch) cubes, then rinsed and patted completely dry

500 g (1 lb 2 oz) ripe Roma (plum) tomatoes

2 tablespoons olive oil, extra

¹/₄ red onion, finely chopped

2 garlic cloves, crushed

3 teaspoons paprika

¹/₄ teaspoon cayenne pepper

1 bay leaf

1 teaspoon sugar

1 tablespoon chopped flat-leaf (Italian) parsley

1 Fill a deep-fryer or large heavy-based saucepan one-third full of oil and heat to 180°C (350°F), or until a cube of bread dropped in the oil browns in 15 seconds. Cook the potato in batches for 10 minutes, or until golden. Drain on crumpled paper towels. Do not discard the oil.

2 Score a cross in the base of each tomato. Place in a bowl of boiling water for 1 minute, then plunge into cold water and peel the skin away from the cross. Chop the flesh.

3 Heat the extra olive oil in a saucepan, add the onion and cook over medium heat for 3 minutes, or until soft and golden. Add the garlic, paprika and cayenne and cook for 1−2 minutes. Add the tomato, bay leaf, sugar and 100 ml (3¹/₂ fl oz) water and cook, stirring occasionally, for 20 minutes. Cool slightly, remove the bay leaf, then process in a food processor until smooth, adding a little water if needed. Prior to serving, reheat the sauce over low heat. Season well.

4 Reheat the oil to 180°C (350°F). Recook the potato in batches for 2 minutes, or until crisp. Drain. Place the potatoes on a platter and pour over the sauce. Garnish with parsley.

INGREDIENTS

500 g (2¼ cups) chickpeas
2 tablespoons oil or ghee
2 large red onions, thinly sliced
2 cm (¾ inch) piece of ginger, finely chopped
2 teaspoons sugar
2 teaspoons ground coriander (cilantro)
2 teaspoons ground cumin
pinch of chilli powder (optional)
1 teaspoon garam masala
3 tablespoons tamarind purée (see note)
4 ripe tomatoes, chopped
4 tablespoons coriander (cilantro) or mint leaves, finely chopped

1   Soak the chickpeas overnight in 2 litres (8 cups) water. Drain, then put the chickpeas in a large saucepan with 2 litres (8 cups) water. Bring to the boil, spooning off any scum from the surface. Cover and simmer over low heat for 1–1½ hours until soft. It is important they are soft at this stage as they won't soften any more once the sauce has been added. Drain.

2   Heat the oil in a heavy-based frying pan. Fry the onion until soft and brown, then stir in the ginger. Add the chickpeas, sugar, coriander, cumin, chilli powder, garam masala and a pinch of salt. Stir, then add the tamarind and tomato and simmer for 2–3 minutes. Add 500 ml (2 cups) water, bring to the boil and cook until the sauce has thickened. Stir in the coriander leaves. Serve with Indian bread such as rotis or naan.

NOTE   Tamarind is a souring agent made from the pods of the tamarind tree. It is sold as a block of pulp (including husks and seeds), as cleaned pulp, or as ready-prepared tamarind purée or concentrate.

INGREDIENTS

4 large unpeeled potatoes, halved
600 g (1lb 5 oz) unpeeled orange sweet potatoes (kumera), halved
20 g ($^3/_4$ oz) butter
1 tablespoon olive oil
2 large leeks, thinly sliced
3 garlic cloves, crushed
6 zucchini (courgettes), thinly sliced on the diagonal
300 ml (10$^1/_2$ fl oz) cream
130 g (1 cup) grated Parmesan cheese
1 tablespoon finely chopped thyme
1 tablespoon chopped flat-leaf (Italian) parsley
130 g (1 cup) grated Cheddar cheese

1   Preheat the oven to 180°C (350°F/ Gas 4) and grease a deep 2.5 litre (10 cup) ovenproof dish. Boil the potato and sweet potato for 10 minutes.

2   Meanwhile, heat the butter and oil in a frying pan. Add the leek and cook over low heat for 4–5 minutes, or until softened. Add 1 garlic clove and the zucchini and cook for 3–4 minutes, or until the zucchini starts to soften. Combine the cream, Parmesan, herbs and remaining garlic and season.

3   When the potatoes and sweet potatoes are cool, peel off the skins and thinly slice. Layer half the potato slices in the base of the dish. Season. Spread with a quarter of the cream mixture, then cover with the zucchini mixture, patting down well. Top with another quarter of the cream mixture. Use all the sweet potato slices to make another layer, and cover with half of the remaining cream mixture. Top with the remaining potato slices, then the last of the cream mixture. Season and top with the Cheddar.

4   Bake for 1$^1/_4$ hours, or until the vegetables are cooked. Cover with a tented sheet of foil towards the end if the top starts over-browning. Stand for 10 minutes before cutting.

750 g (1¹/₂ lb) waxy or all-purpose potatoes (see note)
1 onion
1 cup (125 g/4 oz) grated Cheddar
1¹/₂ cups (375 ml/12 fl oz) cream
2 teaspoons chicken stock powder

1 Preheat the oven to moderate 180°C (350°F/Gas 4). Peel the potatoes and thinly slice them. Peel the onion and slice it into rings.

2 Arrange a layer of overlapping potato slices in the base of a large casserole dish. Top the potato slices with a layer of the onion rings. Divide the grated cheese in half and set aside one half to use as a topping. Sprinkle a little of the remaining grated cheese over the onion rings. Continue layering in this order until all the potato and the onion have been used, finishing with a little of the grated cheese.

3 Pour the cream into a small jug, add the chicken stock powder and whisk gently until the mixture is thoroughly combined. Carefully pour the mixture over the layered potato and onion slices, and sprinkle the top with the reserved grated cheese. Bake the casserole, uncovered, for 40 minutes, or until the potato is tender, the cheese has melted and the top is golden brown.

NOTE If you prefer, you can use different types of stock, including vegetable, to vary the flavour. Waxy or all-purpose potatoes are best to use in this recipe because they hold their shape better when slow-cooked. If you have a mandolin, use it to cut the potatoes into slices. If not, make sure you use a very sharp knife. Peel the skin very thinly.

CREAMY POTATO CASSEROLE

INGREDIENTS

2 tablespoons oil
2 onions, chopped
1 teaspoon ground ginger
2 teaspoons ground paprika
2 teaspoons ground cumin
1 cinnamon stick
pinch of saffron threads
1.5 kg (3 lb) vegetables, peeled and cut into large chunks (carrot, eggplant, orange sweet potato, parsnip, potato, pumpkin)
½ preserved lemon, rinsed, pith and flesh removed, thinly sliced
400 g (13 oz) can peeled tomatoes
1 cup (250 ml/8 fl oz) vegetable stock
100 g (3½ oz) dried pears, halved
60 g (2 oz) pitted prunes
2 zucchini (courgettes), cut into large chunks
300 g (10 oz) instant couscous
1 tablespoon olive oil
3 tablespoons chopped fresh flat-leaf parsley
⅓ cup (50 g/1¾ oz) almonds

1   Preheat the oven to moderate 180°C (350°F/Gas 4). Heat the oil in a large saucepan or ovenproof dish, add the onion and cook over medium heat for 5 minutes, or until soft. Add the spices and cook for 3 minutes.

2   Add the vegetables and cook, stirring, until coated with the spices and the outside begins to soften. Add the lemon, tomatoes, stock, pears and prunes. Cover, transfer to the oven and cook for 30 minutes. Add the zucchini and cook for 15–20 minutes, or until the vegetables are tender.

3   Cover the couscous with the olive oil and 2 cups (500 ml/16 fl oz) boiling water and leave until all the water has been absorbed. Flake with a fork.

4   Remove the cinnamon stick from the vegetables, then stir in the parsley. Serve on a large platter with the couscous formed into a ring and the vegetable tagine in the centre, sprinkled with the almonds.

600 g (1 lb 5 oz) peeled and seeded pumpkin, cut into 3 cm (1¼ inch) cubes

2 tablespoons oil

1 tablespoon ready-made red curry paste

400 ml (14 fl oz) coconut cream

200 g (7 oz) green beans, cut into 3 cm (1¼ inch) lengths

2 kaffir lime (makrut) leaves, crushed

1 tablespoon grated light palm sugar or soft brown sugar

1 tablespoon fish sauce

30 g (1 cup) Thai basil leaves, plus extra, to garnish

1 tablespoon lime juice

1 Preheat the oven to 200°C (400°F/Gas 6). Place the pumpkin in a baking dish with 1 tablespoon of the oil and toss to coat. Bake for 20 minutes, or until tender.

2 Heat the remaining oil in a saucepan, add the curry paste and cook, stirring constantly, breaking up with a fork, over medium heat for 1–2 minutes. Add the coconut cream 125 ml (½ cup) at a time, stirring well with a wooden spoon between each addition for a creamy consistency. Add the pumpkin and any roasting juices, the beans and lime leaves. Reduce the heat to low and cook for 5 minutes.

3 Stir in the palm sugar, fish sauce, basil and lime juice. Garnish with extra basil leaves. Serve with rice.

RED CURRY OF ROAST PUMPKIN, BEANS AND BASIL

INGREDIENTS

1 cup (220 g/7 oz) dried chickpeas
2 tablespoons oil
2 onions, finely chopped
2 large ripe tomatoes, chopped
$^1/_2$ teaspoon ground coriander (cilantro)
1 teaspoon ground cumin
1 teaspoon chilli powder
$^1/_4$ teaspoon ground turmeric
1 tablespoon channa (chole) masala (see note)
20 g ($^3/_4$ oz) ghee or butter
1 small white onion, sliced
fresh mint and coriander (cilantro) leaves, to garnish

1   Place the chickpeas in a bowl, cover with water and leave to soak overnight. Drain, rinse and place in a large saucepan. Cover with plenty of water and bring to the boil, then reduce the heat and simmer for 40 minutes, or until soft. Drain.

2   Heat the oil in a large saucepan, add the onion and cook over medium heat for 15 minutes, or until golden brown. Add the tomato, ground coriander and cumin, chilli powder, turmeric, channa (chole) masala and 2 cups (500 ml/16 fl oz) cold water, and cook for 10 minutes, or until the tomato is soft. Add the chickpeas, season well with salt and cook for 7–10 minutes, or until the sauce thickens. Transfer to a serving dish. Place the ghee or butter on top and allow to melt before serving. Garnish with sliced onion and fresh mint and coriander leaves.

NOTE   Channa (chole) masala is a spice blend specifically used in this dish. It is available at Indian grocery stores. Garam masala can be used as a substitute, but this will alter the final flavour.

INGREDIENTS

Curry paste

10 small fresh red chillies

50 g (1³/₄ oz) red Asian shallots, peeled

1 tablespoon finely chopped coriander (cilantro) stem and root

1 stem lemon grass (white part only), chopped

2 tablespoons grated fresh galangal

2 cloves garlic

1 tablespoon ground coriander (cilantro)

1 teaspoon ground cumin

1 teaspoon black peppercorns

¹/₂ teaspoon ground turmeric

1 tablespoon lime juice

1 tablespoon oil

1 onion, finely chopped

2 cups (500 ml/16 fl oz) coconut milk

200 g (6¹/₂ oz) fried tofu puffs, halved on the diagonal

fresh coriander (cilantro) sprigs, to garnish

1   To make the curry paste, place all the ingredients in a food processor or spice grinder and process until smooth.

2   Heat the oil in a large saucepan, add the onion and cook over medium heat for 4–5 minutes, or until starting to brown. Add 3 tablespoons of the curry paste and cook, stirring, for 2 minutes.

3   Stir in the coconut milk and ¹/₂ cup (125 ml/4 fl oz) water, and season with salt. Bring slowly to the boil, stirring constantly. Add the tofu puffs, then reduce the heat and simmer, stirring frequently, for 5 minutes, or until the sauce thickens slightly. Garnish with the fresh coriander sprigs.

INGREDIENTS

Curry paste
4 cardamom pods
1 teaspoon grated fresh ginger
2 cloves garlic
6 small fresh red chillies
1 teaspoon cumin seeds
1/4 cup (40 g/1 1/4 oz) raw cashew nut pieces
1 tablespoon white poppy seeds (khus) (see note)
1 cinnamon stick
6 cloves

1 kg (2 lb) potatoes, cubed
2 onions, roughly chopped
2 tablespoons oil
1/2 teaspoon ground turmeric
1 teaspoon besan (chickpea flour)
1 cup (250 g/8 oz) plain yoghurt
fresh coriander (cilantro) leaves, to garnish

1 To make the curry paste, lightly crush the cardamom pods with the flat side of a heavy knife. Remove the seeds, discarding the pods. Place the seeds and the remaining curry paste ingredients in a food processor, and process to a smooth paste.

2 Bring a large saucepan of lightly salted water to the boil. Add the potato and cook for 5–6 minutes, or until just tender. Drain.

3 Place the onion in a food processor and process in short bursts until it is finely ground but not puréed. Heat the oil in a large saucepan, add the ground onion and cook over low heat for 5 minutes. Add the curry paste and cook, stirring, for a further 5 minutes, or until fragrant. Stir in the potato, turmeric, salt to taste and 1 cup (250 ml/8 fl oz) water.

4 Reduce the heat and simmer, tightly covered, for 10 minutes, or until the potato is cooked but not breaking up and the sauce has thickened slightly.

5 Combine the besan with the yoghurt, add to the potato mixture and cook, stirring, over low heat for 5 minutes, or until thickened again. Garnish with the coriander leaves.

NOTE White poppy seeds (khus) should not be mistaken for black and do not yield opium. They are off-white, odourless and flavourless until roasted when they have a slight sesame aroma and flavour. If they are not available, replace the poppy seeds with sesame seeds.

INGREDIENTS

Curry paste
10 small fresh green chillies
50 g (1¾ oz) red Asian shallots, peeled
2 cloves garlic
1 cup (50 g/1¾ oz) finely chopped coriander (cilantro)
   stems and roots
1 stem lemon grass (white part only), chopped
2 tablespoons grated fresh galangal
1 tablespoon ground coriander (cilantro)
1 teaspoon ground cumin
1 teaspoon black peppercorns
1/2 teaspoon ground turmeric
1 tablespoon lime juice

2 tablespoons oil
1 onion, sliced
400 ml (13 fl oz) can coconut cream
4–5 kaffir lime (makrut) leaves, torn
500 g (1 lb) firm tofu, cut into 2 cm (¾ inch) cubes
1 tablespoon lime juice
1 tablespoon shredded fresh Thai basil

1 To make the curry paste, place all the ingredients in a food processor and process until smooth.

2 Heat the oil in a frying pan, add the onion and cook for 5 minutes, or until soft. Add 4 tablespoons curry paste (or more for a stronger flavour) and cook, stirring, for 2 minutes. Stir in the coconut cream and 1 cup (250 ml/8 fl oz) water, and season with salt. Bring to the boil and add the lime leaves and tofu. Reduce the heat and simmer for 8 minutes, stirring often. Stir in the lime juice and Thai basil, and serve.

NOTE The recipe for the curry paste makes 1 cup, but you will only need ⅓ cup. Freeze the remaining paste in two portions to use at a later date.

GREEN TOFU CURRY

INGREDIENTS

Curry paste
5 candlenuts
75 g (2¹/₂ oz) red Asian shallots
2 cloves garlic
2 teaspoons sambal oelek
¹/₄ teaspoon ground turmeric
1 teaspoon grated fresh galangal
1 tablespoon peanut butter

2 tablespoons oil
1 onion, sliced
400 ml (13 fl oz) can coconut cream
200 g (6¹/₂ oz) carrots, julienned
200 g (6¹/₂ oz) snake beans, cut into 7 cm (2³/₄ inch) lengths
300 g (10 oz) Chinese cabbage, roughly shredded
100 g (3¹/₂ oz) fresh shiitake mushrooms
¹/₄ teaspoon sugar

1 To make the curry paste, place the candlenuts, red Asian shallots, garlic, sambal oelek, turmeric, galangal and peanut butter in a food processor, and process to a smooth paste.

2 Heat the oil in a large saucepan over low heat. Cook the curry paste, stirring, for 5 minutes, or until fragrant. Add the onion and cook for 5 minutes. Stir in ¹/₄ cup (60 ml/2 fl oz) coconut cream and cook, stirring constantly, for 2 minutes, or until thickened. Add the carrot and snake beans, and cook over high heat for 3 minutes. Stir in the Chinese cabbage, mushrooms and 1 cup (250 ml/8 fl oz) water. Cook over high heat for 8–10 minutes, or until the vegetables are nearly cooked.

3 Stir in the remaining coconut cream and the sugar, and season to taste with salt. Bring to the boil, stirring constantly, then reduce the heat and simmer for 8–10 minutes to allow the flavours to develop. Serve hot.

INGREDIENTS

Paneer
2 litres full-cream milk
1/3 cup (80 ml/23/4 fl oz) lemon juice
oil, for deep-frying

Curry paste
2 large onions
3 cloves garlic
1 teaspoon grated fresh ginger
1 teaspoon cumin seeds
3 dried red chillies
1 teaspoon cardamom seeds
4 cloves
1 teaspoon fennel seeds
2 pieces cassia bark

500 g (1 lb) frozen peas
2 tablespoons oil
400 g (13 oz) tomato paste (purée)
1 tablespoon garam masala
1 teaspoon ground coriander (cilantro)
$^1/_4$ teaspoon ground turmeric
1 tablespoon cream
fresh coriander leaves, to garnish

1 Place the milk in a large saucepan, bring to the boil, stir in the lemon juice and turn off the heat. Stir the mixture for 1–2 seconds as it curdles. Place in a colander and leave for 30 minutes for the whey to drain off. Place the paneer curds on a clean, flat surface, cover with a plate, weigh down and leave for at least 4 hours.

2 To make the curry paste, place the ingredients in a spice grinder or mortar and pestle, and grind to a smooth paste.

3 Cut the solid paneer into 2 cm ($^3/_4$ inch) cubes. Fill a deep heavy-based saucepan one-third full of oil and heat to 180°C (350°F), or until a cube of bread browns in 15 seconds. Cook the paneer in batches for 2–3 minutes, or until golden. Drain on paper towels.

4 Cook the peas in a saucepan of boiling water for 3 minutes, or until tender. Drain.

5 Heat the oil in a large saucepan, add the curry paste and cook over medium heat for 4 minutes, or until fragrant. Add the tomato purée, spices, cream and $^1/_2$ cup (125 ml/4 fl oz) water. Season with salt, and simmer over medium heat for 5 minutes. Add the paneer and peas, and cook for 3 minutes. Garnish with fresh coriander leaves, and serve hot.

INGREDIENTS

Curry paste

1 tablespoon oil
1 teaspoon coriander (cilantro) seeds
1 teaspoon cumin seeds
8 cloves
1/2 teaspoon fennel seeds
seeds from 4 cardamom pods
6 red Asian shallots, chopped
3 cloves garlic, chopped
1 teaspoon finely chopped lemon grass (white part only)
1 teaspoon finely chopped fresh galangal
4 large dried red chillies
1 teaspoon ground nutmeg
1 teaspoon white pepper

1 tablespoon oil
250 g (8 oz) baby onions
500 g (1 lb) small new potatoes
300 g (10 oz) carrots, cut into 3 cm (1 1/4 inch) pieces
225 g (7 oz) can whole champignons, drained
1 cinnamon stick
1 kaffir lime (makrut) leaf
1 bay leaf
1 cup (250 ml/8 fl oz) coconut cream
1 tablespoon lime juice
3 teaspoons grated palm sugar or soft brown sugar
1 tablespoon shredded fresh Thai basil leaves
1 tablespoon crushed roasted peanuts
fresh Thai basil leaves, extra, to garnish

1   To make the curry paste, heat the oil in a frying pan over low heat, add the coriander, cumin, cloves, fennel seeds and cardamom seeds, and cook for 1–2 minutes, or until fragrant. Place in a food processor and add the shallots, garlic, lemon grass, galangal, chillies, nutmeg and white pepper. Process until smooth, adding a little water as necessary.

2   Heat the oil in a large saucepan, add the curry paste and cook, stirring, over medium heat for 2 minutes, or until fragrant. Add the vegetables, cinnamon stick, kaffir lime leaf and bay leaf, and season with salt. Add enough water to cover—about 2 cups (500 ml/16 fl oz)— and bring to the boil. Reduce the heat and simmer, covered, stirring frequently, for 30–35 minutes, or until the vegetables are cooked. Stir in the coconut cream and cook, uncovered, for 4 minutes, stirring frequently, until thickened slightly. Stir in the lime juice, palm sugar and shredded Thai basil. Add a little water if the sauce is too dry. Garnish with the peanuts and Thai basil leaves.

INGREDIENTS

250 g (8 oz) potatoes, diced
250 g (8 oz) pumpkin, diced
200 g (6½ oz) cauliflower, broken into florets
150 g (5 oz) yellow squash, cut into quarters
1 tablespoon oil
2 onions, chopped
3 tablespoons curry powder
400 g (13 oz) can crushed tomatoes
1 cup (250 ml/8 fl oz) vegetable stock
150 g (5 oz) green beans, cut into short lengths
⅓ cup (90 g/3 oz) natural yoghurt
¼ cup (30 g/1 oz) sultanas

1   Bring a saucepan of water to the boil, add the potato and pumpkin, and cook for 6 minutes, then remove. Add the cauliflower and squash, cook for 4 minutes, then remove.

2   Heat the oil in a large saucepan, add the onion and cook, stirring, over medium heat for 8 minutes, or until starting to brown.

3   Add the curry powder and stir for 1 minute, or until fragrant. Stir in the crushed tomato and vegetable stock.

4   Add the parboiled potato, pumpkin, cauliflower and squash and cook for 5 minutes, then add the green beans and cook for a further 2–3 minutes, or until the vegetables are just tender.

5   Add the yoghurt and sultanas, and stir to combine. Simmer for 3 minutes, or until thickened slightly. Season to taste and serve with lemon wedges.

YELLOW VEGETABLE CURRY

INGREDIENTS

1/4 cup (60 ml/2 fl oz) oil
1 onion, finely chopped
2 tablespoons yellow curry paste
250 g (8 oz) potato, diced
200 g (6 1/2 oz) zucchini (courgette), diced
150 g (5 oz) red capsicum (pepper), diced
100 g (3 1/2 oz) beans, trimmed
50 g (1 3/4 oz) bamboo shoots, sliced
1 cup (250 ml/8 fl oz) vegetable stock
400 ml (13 fl oz) can coconut cream
fresh Thai basil leaves, to garnish

1 Heat the oil in a large saucepan, add the onion and cook over medium heat for 4–5 minutes, or until softened and just turning golden. Add the yellow curry paste and cook, stirring, for 2 minutes, or until fragrant.

2 Add all the vegetables and cook, stirring, over high heat for 2 minutes. Pour in the vegetable stock, reduce the heat to medium and cook, covered, for 15–20 minutes, or until the vegetables are tender. Cook, uncovered, over high heat for 5–10 minutes, or until the sauce has reduced slightly.

3 Stir in the coconut cream, and season with salt. Bring to the boil, stirring frequently, then reduce the heat and simmer for 5 minutes. Garnish with the Thai basil leaves.

4 large potatoes
2 vine-ripened tomatoes, seeded and chopped
125 g can corn kernels, drained
2 spring onions, chopped
1 tablespoon lime juice
$^{1}/_{2}$ teaspoon sugar
1 avocado, diced
$^{1}/_{4}$ cup (15 g) chopped fresh coriander (cilantro) leaves
1 tablespoon sour cream, optional

1   Preheat the oven to hot 210°C (415°F/Gas 6–7). Pierce the potatoes all over with a fork. Bake directly on the oven rack for 1 hour, or until tender when tested with a skewer. Leave for about 2 minutes. Cut a cross in the top of each potato and squeeze gently from the base to open (if the potato is still too hot, hold the potato in a clean tea towel).

2   While the potatoes are cooking, put the tomatoes, corn kernels, spring onions, lime juice and sugar in a bowl and mix well. Add the avocado and coriander leaves. Season. Spoon some mixture onto each potato and, if desired, dollop with the sour cream.

NOTE   These potatoes can be prepared for cooking very quickly. You can also do a chicken topping. Cook 2 chicken breasts in 2 cups (500 ml) boiling chicken stock for 5 minutes. Remove from the heat and cool in the liquid. Shred the meat. Add 2 tablespoons mayonnaise, 1 teaspoon grated lemon rind and 1 tablespoon baby capers. Toss 3 cups (135 g) shredded rocket with 1 tablespoon extra virgin olive oil, 1 tablespoon balsamic vinegar and 1 sliced avocado. Place some in each potato and top with the chicken mixture. Season to taste.

BROWN RICE AND CASHEW PATTIES WITH CORIANDER SAMBAL

INGREDIENTS

250 g dried chickpeas
3 cups (650 g/1 lb 5 oz) instant brown rice
1 tablespoon oil
1 onion, finely chopped
125 g (4 oz) roasted cashew paste
1 egg
60 g (2 oz) tahini
1 teaspoon ground cumin
1 teaspoon ground turmeric
1 tablespoon lemon juice
1 vegetable stock cube
5 tablespoons tamari
1 small carrot, grated
$^1/_2$ cup (40 g/1$^1/_2$ oz) fresh wholemeal breadcrumbs
oil, for shallow-frying
2 tablespoons oil, extra
310 g (10 oz) bok choy, trimmed and washed

Coriander and coconut sambal
90 g (3 oz) fresh coriander (cilantro) leaves
1 clove garlic, chopped
1 small fresh green chilli, seeded and finely chopped
1 teaspoon garam masala
2 tablespoons lime juice
$^1/_4$ cup (15 g/$^1/_2$ oz) shredded coconut

1 Soak the chickpeas in cold water overnight. Drain. Place in a large saucepan and cover with water. Bring to the boil and cook for 1–1$^1/_2$ hours, or until cooked. Drain, reserving 2 table-spoons of the liquid.

2 Meanwhile, bring a saucepan of water to the boil and cook the rice over medium heat for 10–12 minutes, or until tender. Rinse well and drain. Keep warm.

3 Heat the oil in a frying pan and cook the onion for 2–3 minutes, or until golden. Set aside.

4 Mix the chickpeas, cashew paste, egg, tahini, cumin, turmeric, lemon juice, stock cube, reserved chickpea liquid and 2 tablespoons of the tamari in a food processor until smooth. Transfer to a large bowl and add the rice, onion, carrot and breadcrumbs and mix well. Divide the mixture into 16 even portions and form into patties about 1.5 cm thick. Refrigerate for 30 minutes.

5 To make the sambal, finely chop all the ingredients in a food processor. Refrigerate until ready to use.

6 To cook the patties, heat the oil in a large deep frying pan over medium heat and cook in batches for 3–4 minutes each side, or until golden and cooked through. Remove and keep warm. Wipe with a paper towel. In the same pan, heat the extra oil and add the bok choy and cook, tossing, for 1–2 minutes, or until wilted. Pour on the remaining 3 tablespoons tamari and toss through. Place the bok choy on eight serving plates and top with two patties. Spoon a dollop of chilled sambal on top and serve immediately.

INGREDIENTS

350 g (12 oz) savoy cabbage, roughly chopped
175 g (6 oz) potatoes, cut into 2 cm ($^3/_4$ inch) cubes
500 g (1 lb 2 oz) buckwheat pasta (pizzoccheri)
4 tablespoons extra virgin olive oil
1 small bunch sage, finely chopped
2 garlic cloves, finely chopped
350 g (12 oz) mixed cheeses (such as mascarpone, fontina, Taleggio and Gorgonzola)
grated Parmesan cheese, to serve

1   Bring a large saucepan of salted water to the boil. Add the cabbage, potato and the pasta
    and cook for 3–5 minutes, or until the pasta and vegetables are cooked through. Drain,
    reserving about a cup of the cooking water.

2   Dry the saucepan, then add the olive oil and gently cook the sage and garlic for 1 minute.
    Add the mixed cheeses to the pan. Mix briefly, and add the pasta, cabbage and potatoes.
    Season with salt and pepper.

3   Remove the saucepan from the heat and gently stir the mixture together, adding some of
    the reserved pasta water to loosen it up a little if necessary. Serve with Parmesan
    sprinkled over the top.

NOTE   Buckwheat pasta is called pizzoccheri in Italy. This type of pasta is popular in Valtellina,
       near the Swiss border, and is traditionally served with potatoes, cabbage and cheese.

CHICKPEA PATTIES WITH CARAMELIZED ONION

INGREDIENTS

1 tablespoon olive oil
1 red onion, finely chopped
2 cloves garlic, crushed
1 tablespoon ground cumin
2 x 310 g (10 oz) cans chickpeas
¼ cup (30 g/1 oz) sunflower seeds
½ cup (30 g/1 oz) finely chopped fresh coriander (cilantro) leaves
2 eggs, lightly beaten
⅔ cup (75 g/2½ oz) besan flour
oil, for shallow-frying

Caramelized onion
40 g (1¼ oz) butter
2 red onions, thinly sliced
3 teaspoons soft brown sugar
plain yoghurt, to serve

1   Heat the oil in a frying pan, add the onion and cook over medium heat for 3 minutes, or until soft. Add the garlic and cumin and cook for 1 minute. Allow to cool slightly.

2   Blend the drained chickpeas, sunflower seeds, coriander, egg and onion mixture in a food processor until smooth. Fold in the besan flour and season. Divide the mixture into eight portions and, using floured hands, form into patties. Heat 1 cm (½ inch) oil in a frying pan and cook the patties in two batches over medium heat for 2–3 minutes each side, or until firm. Drain on paper towels. Keep warm.

3   To make the caramelized onion, melt the butter in a small frying pan and cook the onion over medium heat for 10 minutes, stirring occasionally. Add the sugar and cook for 1 minute, or until caramelized. Spoon over the patties with a dollop of yoghurt.

NOTE   Besan flour is also known as chickpea flour.

INGREDIENTS

1 cup (185 g/6 oz) couscous
4 tablespoons oil
1 eggplant (aubergine), finely diced
1 onion, finely chopped
1 clove garlic, crushed
2 teaspoons ground cumin
2 teaspoons ground coriander (cilantro)
1 red capsicum (pepper), finely diced
2 tablespoons chopped fresh coriander (cilantro)
2 teaspoons grated lemon rind
2 teaspoons lemon juice
5 tablespoons natural yoghurt
1 egg, lightly beaten
oil, for shallow-frying

1 Place the couscous in a bowl. Add 1 cup (250 ml/8 fl oz) of boiling water and leave for 10 minutes, or until all the water has been absorbed. Fluff up the grains with a fork.

2 Heat 2 tablespoons of the oil in a large frying pan and fry the eggplant until soft and golden, then place in a bowl. Heat 1 tablespoon of the oil in the pan. Add the onion, garlic, cumin and ground coriander. Cook over medium heat for 3–4 minutes, or until soft, then add to the bowl. Heat the remaining oil and cook the capsicum for 5 minutes, or until soft. Place in the bowl and stir well.

3 Add the vegetable mixture to the couscous with the fresh coriander, lemon rind, lemon juice, yoghurt and egg. Season to taste and mix well.

4 Using damp hands, divide the mixture into four portions and form into large patties—they should be about 2 cm (¾ inch) thick. Cover and refrigerate for 15 minutes. Shallow-fry the patties over medium heat for 5 minutes on each side, or until golden. Drain the patties well and serve with yoghurt.

COUSCOUS PATTIES

INGREDIENTS

1 litre (32 fl oz) vegetable stock
500 g (1 lb) instant couscous
30 g (1 oz) butter
3 tablespoons olive oil
2 cloves garlic, crushed
1 onion, finely chopped
1 tablespoon ground coriander (cilantro)
1 teaspoon ground cinnamon
1 teaspoon garam masala
250 g (8 oz) cherry tomatoes, quartered
1 zucchini (courgette), diced
130 g (4½ oz) can corn kernels, drained
8 large fresh basil leaves
150 g (5 oz) sun-dried capsicums (peppers) in oil
1 cup (60 g/2 oz) chopped fresh basil
⅓ cup (80 ml/2¾ fl oz) orange juice
1 tablespoon lemon juice
3 tablespoons chopped fresh flat-leaf parsley
1 teaspoon honey
1 teaspoon ground cumin

1 Bring the stock to the boil. Put the couscous and butter in a bowl, cover with the stock; leave for 10 minutes.

2 Heat 1 tablespoon of the oil in a large frying pan and cook the garlic and onion over low heat for 5 minutes, or until the onion is soft. Add the spices and cook for 1 minute, or until fragrant. Remove from the pan.

3 Add the remaining oil to the pan and cook the tomatoes, zucchini and corn over high heat until soft.

4 Line a 3 litre (96 fl oz) loaf tin with plastic wrap, letting it overhang the sides. Arrange the basil leaves in the shape of two flowers in the base of the tin. Drain the capsicums, reserving 2 tablespoons of the oil, then roughly chop. Add the onion mixture, tomato mixture, capsicum and chopped basil to the couscous and mix. Cool.

5 Press into the tin and fold the plastic wrap over to cover. Weigh down with cans of food to compress the loaf and refrigerate overnight.

6 To make the dressing, put the remaining ingredients and reserved capsicum oil in a screw-top jar and shake. Turn out the loaf, cut into slices and serve with the dressing.

INGREDIENTS

3 large red capsicums (peppers)
1 large potato, halved
40 g (1¼ oz) butter
2 cloves garlic, crushed
800 g (1 lb 10 oz) English spinach leaves, shredded
¼ cup (60 ml/2 fl oz) cream
1 egg yolk
⅓ cup (80 ml/23/4 fl oz) olive oil
2 eggplants, cut into 5 mm (¼ inch) slices lengthways
1 cup (30 g/1 oz) fresh basil
350 g (11 oz) ricotta cheese
2 cloves garlic, crushed, extra

1   Cut the capsicums into large pieces, removing the seeds and membranes. Cook, skin-side-up, under a hot grill until the skin blisters. Cool, then peel.

2   Preheat the oven to moderate 180°C (350°F/Gas 4). Grease a 1.5 litre (48 fl oz) terrine and line with baking paper. Bring a saucepan of salted water to the boil and cook the potato for 10 minutes. Drain and cool. Cut into 5 mm (¼ inch) slices.

3   Melt the butter in a large saucepan and cook the garlic for 30 seconds. Add the spinach and toss. Steam, covered, over low heat for 2–3 minutes, or until wilted. Cool slightly and place in a food processor or blender and process until smooth. Squeeze out any excess liquid, put in a bowl and stir in the cream and egg.

4   Heat a chargrill plate over high heat and brush with some of the oil. Cook the eggplant for 2–3 minutes each side, or until golden, brushing with the remaining oil while cooking.

5   To assemble, arrange one third of the eggplant neatly in the base of the terrine, cutting to fit. Top with a layer of half the capsicum, spinach mixture, basil, all the potato, and all the combined ricotta and garlic. Repeat with the remaining ingredients, finishing with eggplant. Oil a piece of foil and cover the terrine, sealing well. Place in a baking dish and half-fill with water. Bake for 25–30 minutes. Remove from the oven, put a piece of cardboard on top and weigh the terrine down with weights or small food cans. Refrigerate overnight, then turn out and cut into slices.

INGREDIENTS

10 g (¹/₄ oz) dried shiitake mushrooms
350 g (12 oz) buckwheat (soba) noodles
2 teaspoons sesame oil
3 tablespoons tahini
1 tablespoon light soy sauce
1 tablespoon dark soy sauce
1 tablespoon honey
2 tablespoons lemon juice
3 tablespoons peanut oil
2 long, thin eggplants (aubergines), cut into very thin strips
2 carrots, julienned
10 spring onions (scallions), cut on the diagonal
6 fresh shiitake mushrooms, thinly sliced
50 g (1 cup) roughly chopped coriander (cilantro) leaves

1   Soak the dried shiitake mushrooms in 125 ml (¹/₂ cup) hot water for 10 minutes. Drain, reserving the liquid. Discard the woody stems and finely slice the caps.

2   Cook the noodles in a saucepan of boiling water for 5 minutes, or until tender. Drain. Refresh under cold water, then toss with 1 teaspoon of the sesame oil.

3   Combine the tahini, light and dark soy sauces, honey, lemon juice, 2 tablespoons of the reserved mushroom liquid and the remaining teaspoon of sesame oil in a food processor until smooth.

4   Heat 2 tablespoons of the peanut oil over high heat. Add the eggplant and cook, turning often, for 4–5 minutes, or until soft and golden. Drain on paper towels.

5   Heat the remaining oil. Add the carrot, spring onion and fresh and dried mushrooms. Cook, stirring constantly, for 1–2 minutes, or until just softened. Remove from the heat and toss with the noodles, eggplant and dressing. Garnish with the coriander.

INGREDIENTS

500 g (1 lb 2 oz) ready-made potato gnocchi
walnuts, to garnish
375 ml (1$^1/_2$ cups) cream
200 g (7 oz) mild gorgonzola cheese, crumbled
2 tablespoons grated Parmesan cheese
40 g (1$^1/_2$ oz) butter
pinch of grated nutmeg

1   Cook the gnocchi in a large saucepan of boiling salted water until al dente.

2   Spread the walnuts on a baking tray and toast in a 180°C (350°F/Gas 4) oven for
    5–8 minutes, or until lightly coloured. Alternatively, place them on a tray under a hot grill
    (broiler). Once they start to brown, nuts burn very quickly, so watch them carefully. Cool,
    then roughly chop.

3   Put the cream, gorgonzola, Parmesan and butter in a saucepan and heat over low heat,
    stirring occasionally, for 3 minutes, or until the cheeses have melted into a smooth sauce.

4   Stir in the nutmeg and serve immediately over the hot pasta. Garnish with the walnuts.

NOTE   This dish is very rich and is recommended as a starter rather than a main course.

INGREDIENTS

60 g (2 oz) ghee or butter
2 onions, thinly sliced
2 tablespoons Madras curry paste
2 cloves garlic, crushed
180 g (6 oz) button mushrooms, sliced
1 litre (32 fl oz) vegetable stock
300 g (10 oz) brown or green lentils
400 g (13 oz) can chopped tomatoes
2 cinnamon sticks
300 g (10 oz) cauliflower, cut into small florets
oil, for deep-frying
18 small (8 cm/3 inch) pappadums
plain yoghurt and coriander (cilantro), to serve

1 Heat the ghee in a large pan over medium heat and cook the onion for 2–3 minutes, or until soft. Add the curry paste, garlic and mushrooms and cook for 2 minutes, or until soft.

2 Add the stock, lentils, tomato and cinnamon and mix well. Bring to the boil and cook for 40 minutes, or until the lentils are tender. Add the cauliflower in the last 10 minutes and cover. If the curry is too wet, continue to cook, uncovered, until the excess liquid has evaporated. Season to taste with salt and cracked black pepper. Remove the cinnamon.

3 Meanwhile, fill a deep heavy-based saucepan one third full of oil and heat until a cube of bread dropped into the oil browns in 15 seconds. Cook the pappadums in batches for 10 seconds, or until golden brown and puffed all over. Drain on crumpled paper towels and season with salt.

4 To assemble, place a pappadum on each serving plate and spoon on a little of the curry. Place a second pappadum on top and spoon on some more curry. Cover with the remaining pappadum and top with a spoonful of yoghurt. Garnish with coriander sprigs and serve immediately (the pappadums will become soggy if left to stand for too long.)

INGREDIENTS

3 Lebanese cucumbers, thinly sliced

20 g ($^3/_4$ oz) dried wakame

500 g (1 lb) silken firm tofu, well drained

3 tablespoons shiro miso

1 tablespoon mirin

1 tablespoon sugar

1 tablespoon rice vinegar

1 egg yolk

100 g ($3^1/_2$ oz) bean sprouts, blanched

2 tablespoons sesame seeds, toasted

Dressing

3 tablespoons rice vinegar

$^1/_4$ teaspoon soy sauce

$1^1/_2$ tablespoons sugar

1 tablespoon mirin

1 Sprinkle the cucumber generously with salt and leave for 20 minutes, or until very soft, then rinse and drain. To rehydrate the wakame, place it in a colander in the sink and leave it under cold running water for 10 minutes, then drain well.

2 Place the tofu in a colander, weigh down with a plate and leave to drain.

3 Place the shiro miso, mirin, sugar, rice vinegar and 2 tablespoons water in a saucepan and stir over low heat for 1 minute, or until the sugar dissolves. Remove from the heat, then add the egg yolk and whisk until glossy. Cool slightly.

4 Cut the tofu into thick sticks and place on a non-stick baking tray. Brush the miso mixture over the tofu and cook under a hot grill for 6 minutes each side, or until light golden on both sides.

5 To make the dressing, place all the ingredients and $^1/_2$ teaspoon salt in a bowl and whisk together well.

6 To assemble, place the cucumber in the centre of a plate, top with the sprouts and wakame, drizzle with the dressing, top with tofu and serve sprinkled with the sesame seeds.

ITALIAN ZUCCHINI PIE

600 g (1 lb 5 oz) zucchini (courgettes), grated and mixed with $1/4$ teaspoon salt
150 g ($5^{1}/_{2}$ oz) provolone cheese, grated
120 g ($4^{1}/_{2}$ oz) ricotta cheese
3 eggs
2 garlic cloves, crushed
2 teaspoons finely chopped basil
pinch ground nutmeg
2 sheets ready-rolled shortcrust pastry
1 egg (extra), lightly beaten

1 Preheat the oven to 200°C (400°F/ Gas 6) and heat a baking tray. Grease a 23 cm (9 inch) (top) pie dish. Drain the zucchini in a colander for 30 minutes, then squeeze out any excess liquid. Place in a bowl with the cheeses, eggs, garlic, basil and nutmeg. Season and mix well.

2 Using two-thirds of the pastry, line the base and sides of the dish. Spoon the filling into the pastry shell and level the surface. Brush the exposed rim of the pastry with egg. Use two-thirds of the remaining pastry to make a lid. Cover the filling with it, pressing the edges together firmly. Trim the edges and reserve the scraps. Crimp the rim. Prick the top all over with a skewer and brush with egg.

3 From the remaining pastry, cut a strip about 30 cm x 10 cm (12 inches x 4 inches). Cut this into nine lengths 1 cm ($1/2$ inch) wide. Press three ropes together at one end and press onto the workbench. Plait the ropes. Make two more plaits, trim the ends and space the plaits parallel across the centre of the pie. Brush with egg. Bake on the hot tray for 50 minutes, or until golden.

INGREDIENTS

1 eggplant (250 g/8 oz), cut into 1 cm (½ inch) slices
1 large potato, cut into 1 cm (½ inch) slices
30 g (1 oz) butter
1 onion, finely chopped
2 cloves garlic, finely chopped
500 g (1 lb) flat mushrooms, sliced
400 g (13 oz) can chopped tomatoes
½ teaspoon sugar
40 g (1¼ oz) butter, extra
1/3 cup (40 g/1¼ oz) plain (all-purpose) flour
2 cups (500 ml/16 fl oz) milk
1 egg, lightly beaten
40 g (1¼ oz) grated Parmesan

1 Preheat the oven to hot 220°C (425°F/Gas 7). Line a large baking tray with foil and brush with oil. Put the eggplant and potato in a single layer on the tray and sprinkle with salt and pepper. Bake for 20 minutes.

2 Melt the butter in a large frying pan over medium heat. Add the onion and cook, stirring, for 3–4 minutes, or until soft. Add the garlic and cook for 1 minute, or until fragrant. Increase the heat to high, add the mushrooms and stir continuously for 2–3 minutes, or until soft. Add the tomato, reduce the heat and simmer rapidly for 8 minutes, or until reduced. Stir in the sugar.

3 Melt the extra butter in a large saucepan over low heat. Add the flour and cook for 1 minute, or until pale and foaming. Remove from the heat and gradually stir in the milk. Return to the heat and stir constantly until it boils and thickens. Reduce the heat and simmer for 2 minutes. Remove from the heat and, when the bubbles subside, stir in the egg and Parmesan.

4 Reduce the oven to moderate 180°C (350°F/Gas 4). Grease a shallow 1.5 litre (48 fl oz) ovenproof dish. Spoon one third of the mushroom mixture into the dish. Cover with potato and top with half the remaining mushrooms, then the eggplant. Finish with the remaining mushrooms, pour on the sauce and smooth the top. Bake for 30–35 minutes, or until the edges bubble. Leave for 10 minutes before serving.

INGREDIENTS

1 kg (2 lb 4 oz) pumpkin or butternut pumpkin (squash), cut into 2 cm (³/₄ inch) cubes
80 ml (¹/₃ cup) olive oil
500 g (1 lb 2 oz) orecchiette (see note)
2 garlic cloves, crushed
1 teaspoon dried chilli flakes
1 teaspoon coriander seeds, crushed
1 tablespoon cumin seeds, crushed
185 g (³/₄ cup) thick natural yoghurt
3 tablespoons chopped coriander (cilantro) leaves

1   Preheat the oven to 200°C (400°F/Gas 6). Toss the pumpkin cubes in 2 tablespoons of the oil, place in a roasting tin and cook for 30 minutes, or until golden and crisp, tossing halfway through.

2   Meanwhile, cook the pasta in a large saucepan of boiling salted water until al dente. Drain and return to the pan.

3   Heat the remaining oil in a saucepan. Add the garlic, chilli, coriander and cumin and cook for 30 seconds, or until fragrant. Toss the spice mix and pumpkin through the pasta, then stir in the yoghurt and coriander and season to taste with salt and freshly ground black pepper. Divide among serving bowls.

NOTE   Orecchiette means 'little ears' in Italian, and the name of the pasta is a literal description of the shape — although some brands look more like curls than ears. If unavailable, use conchiglie or cavatelli.

INGREDIENTS

185 ml (³/₄ cup) olive oil
1 onion, finely chopped
2 garlic cloves, finely chopped
2 x 400 g (14 oz) cans chopped tomatoes
400 g (14 oz) bucatini or spaghetti
1 large eggplant (aubergine), about 500 g (1 lb 2 oz)
30 g (¹/₂ cup) basil leaves, torn, plus extra, to garnish
60 g (¹/₂ cup) ricotta salata (see note), crumbled
45 g (¹/₂ cup) grated pecorino or Parmesan cheese
1 tablespoon extra virgin olive oil, to drizzle

1 Heat 2 tablespoons of the oil in a frying pan and cook the onion over medium heat for 5 minutes, or until softened. Stir in the garlic and cook for 30 seconds. Add the tomato and season. Reduce the heat to low and cook for 20–25 minutes, or until the sauce has thickened and reduced.

2 Cook the pasta in a saucepan of boiling salted water until al dente. Meanwhile, cut the eggplant lengthways into 5 mm (¹/₄ inch) thick slices. Heat the remaining olive oil in a large frying pan. When the oil is hot but not smoking, add the eggplant slices a few at a time and cook for 3–5 minutes, or until lightly browned on both sides. Remove from the pan and drain on crumpled paper towels.

3 Add the eggplant to the sauce with the basil, stirring over very low heat.

4 Add the hot pasta to the sauce with half each of the ricotta and pecorino and toss together well. Serve immediately, sprinkled with the remaining cheeses and extra basil and drizzled with oil.

NOTE Ricotta salata is a lightly salted, pressed ricotta cheese. If unavailable, use a mild feta cheese.

INGREDIENTS

1 kg (2 lb 4 oz) butternut pumpkin (squash), peeled and cut into 2 cm ($^3/_4$ inch) chunks
1 red onion, thinly sliced
8 garlic cloves, unpeeled
1 tablespoon rosemary leaves
80 ml ($^1/_3$ cup) olive oil
400 g (14 oz) casserechi pasta, or macaroni, gemelli or other short pasta
200 g (7 oz) marinated feta cheese, crumbled
2 tablespoons grated Parmesan cheese
2 tablespoons finely chopped parsley

1 Preheat the oven to 200°C (400°F/Gas 6). Put the pumpkin, onion, garlic and rosemary in a roasting tin, then drizzle with 1 tablespoon of the oil. Season. Using your hands, rub the oil over all the ingredients until well coated. Roast for 30 minutes, or until the pumpkin is soft and starting to caramelize.

2 Cook the pasta in a saucepan of boiling salted water until al dente.

3 Squeeze the roasted garlic out of its skin and place it in a bowl with the remaining oil. Mash with a fork.

4 Add the garlic oil to the hot pasta, then the remaining ingredients. Toss well and season.

INGREDIENTS

30 g (1 oz) dried porcini mushrooms
1 litre (4 cups) chicken or vegetable stock
100 g (3$^1/_2$ oz) butter
1 onion, finely chopped
250 g (9 oz) mushrooms, sliced
2 garlic cloves, crushed
385 g (1$^3/_4$ cups) risotto rice (arborio, vialone nano or carnaroli)
pinch of ground nutmeg
1 tablespoon finely chopped parsley
45 g (1$^1/_2$ oz) Parmesan cheese, grated

1   Put the porcini in a bowl, cover with 500 ml (2 cups) hot water and leave to soak for
    15 minutes. Squeeze them dry, reserving the soaking liquid. If the porcini are large, roughly
    chop them. Strain the soaking liquid into a saucepan and add enough stock to make up to
    1 litre (4 cups). Heat up and maintain at a low simmer.

2   Melt the butter in a deep heavy-based frying pan and gently cook the onion until soft but
    not browned. Add the mushrooms and porcini and fry for a few minutes. Add the garlic, stir
    briefly, then add the rice and reduce the heat to low. Season and stir to coat the grains of
    rice in the butter.

3   Increase the heat to medium and add a ladleful of the stock. Cook at a fast simmer,
    stirring constantly. When the stock has been absorbed, stir in another ladleful. Continue
    like this for about 20 minutes, or until the rice is creamy and al dente. Add a little more
    stock or water if you need to — every risotto will use a different amount.

4   Stir in the nutmeg, parsley and half the Parmesan, then serve with the rest of the
    Parmesan sprinkled over the top.

INGREDIENTS

200 g (1 cup) basmati rice
500 ml (2 cups) chicken stock
6 tablespoons ghee or oil
5 cardamom pods
5 cm (2 inch) piece of cinnamon stick
6 cloves
8 black peppercorns
4 Indian bay leaves (cassia leaves)
1 onion, finely sliced

1   Wash the rice in a sieve under cold running water until the water from the rice runs clear. Drain.

2   Heat the stock to near boiling point in a saucepan.

3   Meanwhile, heat 2 tablespoons of the ghee over medium heat in a large heavy-based saucepan. Add the cardamom, cinnamon, cloves, peppercorns and bay leaves and fry for 1 minute. Reduce the heat to low, add the rice and stir constantly for 1 minute. Add the heated stock and some salt to the rice and bring rapidly to a boil. Cover and simmer over low heat for 15 minutes. Allow the rice to rest for 10 minutes before uncovering. Lightly fluff up the rice before serving.

4   Meanwhile, heat the remaining ghee in a frying pan over low heat and fry the onion until soft. Increase the heat and fry until the onion is dark brown. Drain on paper towels, then use as a garnish. Serve with casseroles or Indian curries.

6 sheets ready-rolled puff pastry
1.2 kg pumpkin, cut into 6 cm pieces
6 tablespoons sour cream or cream cheese
sweet chilli sauce, to serve

1 Preheat the oven to moderately hot 200°C (400°F/Gas 6). Lightly grease six 10 cm pie dishes. Cut six 15 cm circles from the pastry, carefully place in the prepared dishes and pleat the pastry to fit. Prick the pastry with a fork. Place on a baking tray and bake for 15–20 minutes, or until lightly golden, pressing down any pastry that puffs up. Cool.

2 Meanwhile, steam the pumpkin pieces for about 15 minutes, or until just tender.

3 Place a tablespoon of sour cream in the middle of each pastry shell and pile the pumpkin pieces on top. Season with salt and black pepper and drizzle with sweet chilli sauce to taste. Return to the oven for 5 minutes to heat through. Remove from the tins and serve immediately.

PUMPKIN TARTS

INGREDIENTS

4 large (10 cm/4 inch) field mushrooms
1 tablespoon olive oil
1 red onion, cut into thin wedges
1 clove garlic, crushed
1 cup (200 g/6½ oz) puy lentils
¾ cup (185 ml/6 fl oz) red wine
1¾ cups (440 ml/14 fl oz) vegetable stock
1 tablespoon finely chopped fresh flat-leaf parsley
30 g (1 oz) butter
2 cloves garlic, crushed, extra

Bean puree

1 large potato, cut into chunks
2 tablespoons extra virgin olive oil
400 g (13 oz) can cannellini beans, drained and rinsed
2 large cloves garlic, crushed
1 tablespoon vegetable stock

Red wine sauce

⅔ cup (170 ml/5½ fl oz) red wine
2 tablespoons tomato paste (purée)
1½ cups (375 ml/12 fl oz) vegetable stock
1 tablespoon soft brown sugar

1 Remove the stalks from the mushrooms and chop them. Heat the oil in a large saucepan and cook the onion over medium heat for 2–3 minutes, or until soft. Add the garlic and mushroom stalks and cook for a further 1 minute. Stir in the lentils, wine and stock and bring to the boil. Reduce the heat and simmer, covered, for 20–25 minutes, stirring occasionally, or until reduced and the lentils are cooked through. If the mixture is too wet, remove the lid and boil until slightly thick. Stir in the parsley and keep warm.

2 Meanwhile, to make the bean purée, bring a small saucepan of water to the boil over high heat and cook the potato for 10 minutes, or until tender. Drain and mash with a potato masher or fork until smooth. Stir in half the extra virgin olive oil. Combine the cannellini beans and garlic in a food processor bowl. Add the stock and the remaining oil and process until smooth. Transfer to a bowl and fold in the mashed potato. Keep warm.

3 Melt the butter in a deep frying pan. Add the mushrooms and extra garlic and cook in batches over medium heat for 4 minutes each side, or until tender. Remove and keep warm.

4 To make the red wine sauce, add the red wine to the same frying pan, then scrape the bottom to remove any sediment. Add the combined tomato paste, stock and sugar and bring to the boil. Cook for about 10 minutes, or until reduced and thickened.

5 To assemble, place the mushrooms onto serving plates and top with the bean purée. Spoon on the lentil mixture and drizzle with the red wine sauce. Season and serve immediately.

NOTE The mushrooms tend to shrivel if you keep them warm in the oven—either turn the oven off or find another warm place.

INGREDIENTS

20 g ($^3/_4$ oz) dried porcini mushrooms
1 litre (4 cups) vegetable or chicken stock
2 tablespoons olive oil
1 tablespoon butter
1 small onion, finely chopped
2 garlic cloves, crushed
385 g ($1^3/_4$ cups) risotto rice (arborio, vialone nano or carnaroli)
250 g (9 oz) mushrooms, sliced
pinch of ground nutmeg
40 g ($1^1/_2$ oz) Parmesan cheese, grated
3 tablespoons finely chopped parsley

1   Soak the porcini in 500 ml (2 cups) boiling water for 30 minutes. Drain, reserving the liquid. Chop the porcini and pass the liquid through a fine sieve. Put the vegetable or chicken stock in a saucepan, bring to the boil and then maintain at a low simmer.

2   Heat the oil and butter in a large wide heavy-based saucepan. Cook the onion and garlic until softened but not browned. Add the rice and reduce the heat to low. Season and stir briefly to thoroughly coat the rice. Toss in the fresh mushrooms and nutmeg. Season and cook, stirring, for 1–2 minutes. Add the porcini and the reserved soaking liquid, increase the heat and cook until the liquid has been absorbed.

3   Stir in a ladleful of hot stock and cook over moderate heat, stirring continuously. When the stock has been absorbed, stir in another ladleful. Continue like this for about 20 minutes, until all the stock has been added and the rice is creamy and al dente. (You may not need to use all the stock, or you may need a little extra.) Remove the pan from the heat and stir in the Parmesan and parsley. Season and serve.

INGREDIENTS

3 orange sweet potatoes (kumera) (500 g/1 lb each)
1 tablespoon olive oil
1 large onion, chopped
3 cloves garlic, crushed
2 teaspoons ground cumin
1 teaspoon ground coriander (cilantro)
½ teaspoon chilli powder
400 g (13 oz) can chopped tomatoes
1 cup (250 ml/8 fl oz) vegetable stock
1 large zucchini (courgette), cubed
1 green capsicum (pepper), cubed
310 g (10 oz) can corn kernels, drained
2 x 400 g (13 oz) cans red kidney beans, rinsed and drained
3 tablespoons chopped fresh coriander (cilantro) leaves
light sour cream and grated reduced-fat Cheddar, to serve

1   Preheat the oven to hot 210°C (415°F/Gas 6–7). Rinse the sweet potatoes, then pierce with a small sharp knife. Place them on a baking tray and bake for 1–1½ hours, or until soft when tested with a skewer or sharp knife.

2   Meanwhile, heat the oil in a large saucepan and cook the onion over medium heat for about 5 minutes, stirring occasionally, until very soft and golden. Add the garlic and spices, and cook, stirring, for 1 minute.

3   Add the tomato and stock, stir well, then add the vegetables and beans. Bring to the boil, then reduce the heat and simmer, partially covered, for 20 minutes. Uncover, increase the heat slightly, and cook for a further 10–15 minutes, or until the liquid has reduced and thickened. Stir in the coriander leaves just before serving.

4   To serve, cut the sweet potatoes in half lengthways. Spoon the vegetable mixture over the top. Add a dollop of light sour cream and sprinkle with grated Cheddar cheese.

INGREDIENTS

2 tablespoons oil
4 spring onions, cut into 3 cm lengths
3 cloves garlic, crushed
1 fresh red chilli, seeded and sliced
75 g button mushrooms, quartered
100 g Chinese cabbage, roughly chopped
2 tablespoons soy sauce
1 teaspoon fish sauce
1 tablespoon oyster sauce
$^1/_4$ cup (60 ml) vegetable stock
$^1/_2$ teaspoon grated palm sugar
150 g snow peas (mangetout)
150 g cauliflower, cut into small florets
150 g broccoli, cut into small florets
fresh coriander (cilantro) leaves, chopped, to garnish

1   Heat a wok until very hot, add the oil and swirl to coat. Add the spring onion, garlic and chilli. Stir-fry for 20 seconds. Add the mushrooms and cabbage and stir-fry for 1 minute.

2   Stir in the sauces, stock, palm sugar, snow peas, cauliflower and broccoli. Cook for 2 minutes, or until tender. Garnish with the coriander leaves.

INGREDIENTS

50 ml (1^3/$_4$ fl oz) extra virgin olive oil
1 red onion, cut into thin wedges
600 g (1 lb 5 oz) orange sweet potato (kumera), peeled and cut into 2 cm (^{3}/$_4$ inch) cubes
440 g (2 cups) arborio rice
1.25 litres (5 cups) hot vegetable stock
75 g (^{3}/$_4$ cup) shredded Parmesan cheese
3 tablespoons shredded sage
shaved Parmesan cheese, extra, to garnish

1 Heat 3 tablespoons oil in a large saucepan and cook the onion over medium heat for 2–3 minutes, or until softened. Add the sweet potato and rice and stir until well coated in the oil.

2 Add 125 ml (^{1}/$_2$ cup) hot stock, stirring constantly over medium heat until the liquid is absorbed. Continue adding more stock, 125 ml (^{1}/$_2$ cup) at a time, stirring constantly for 20–25 minutes, or until all the stock is absorbed, the sweet potato is cooked and the rice is tender and creamy.

3 Add the Parmesan and 2 tablespoons of the sage. Season well and stir to combine. Spoon into four bowls and drizzle with the remaining oil. Sprinkle the remaining sage over the top and garnish with shaved Parmesan.

200 g (2 cups) shelled walnuts
20 g ($\frac{1}{3}$ cup) roughly chopped parsley
50 g (1$\frac{3}{4}$ oz) butter
200 ml (7 fl oz) extra virgin olive oil
1 garlic clove, crushed
30 g (1 oz) Parmesan cheese, grated
100 ml (3$\frac{1}{2}$ fl oz) thick (double/heavy) cream
400 g (14 oz) pasta, such as tagliatelle

1 Lightly toast the walnuts in a dry frying pan over moderately high heat for 2 minutes, or until browned. Set aside to cool for 5 minutes.

2 Put the walnuts in a food processor with the parsley and blend until finely chopped. Add the butter and mix together. Gradually pour in the olive oil in a steady stream with the motor running. Add the garlic, Parmesan and cream. Season with salt and black pepper.

3 Cook the pasta in a large saucepan of boiling salted water until al dente. Drain, then toss through the sauce to serve.

TOFU PUFFS WITH MUSHROOMS AND ROUND RICE NOODLES

8 dried shiitake mushrooms
500 g (1 lb 2 oz) fresh round rice noodles
3 litres (12 cups) good-quality chicken stock
1 carrot, thinly sliced on the diagonal
100 g (3$\frac{1}{2}$ oz) fried tofu puffs, cut in half
800 g (1 lb 12 oz) bok choy (pak choi), trimmed and quartered
1–1$\frac{1}{2}$ tablespoons mushroom soy sauce
6 drops sesame oil
ground white pepper, to season
100 g (3$\frac{1}{2}$ oz) enoki mushrooms, ends trimmed

1 Place the shiitake mushrooms in a heatproof bowl, cover with boiling water and soak for 20 minutes. Drain and remove the stems, squeezing out any excess water.

2 Meanwhile, place the noodles in a heatproof bowl, cover with boiling water and soak briefly. Gently separate the noodles with your hands and drain well.

3 Place the chicken stock in a large saucepan, cover and slowly heat over low heat.

4 Add the noodles to the simmering stock along with the carrot, tofu puffs, shiitake mushrooms and bok choy. Cook for 1–2 minutes, or until the carrot and noodles are tender and the bok choy has wilted slightly. Stir in the soy sauce and sesame oil and season to taste with white pepper.

5 Divide the noodles, vegetables, tofu puffs and enoki mushrooms among four serving bowls, ladle the broth on top and serve immediately.

INGREDIENTS

2 x 300 g (10 oz) packets firm tofu

$^1/_2$ cup (125 ml/4 fl oz) freshly squeezed orange juice

1 tablespoon soft brown sugar

1 tablespoon soy sauce

2 tablespoons chopped fresh coriander (cilantro) leaves

2 cloves garlic, crushed

1 teaspoon grated fresh ginger

2–3 tablespoons oil

1 kg (2 lb) baby bok choy, cut into quarters lengthways

Carrot and ginger sauce

300 g (10 oz) carrots, chopped

2 teaspoons grated fresh ginger

$^2/_3$ cup (170 ml/5$^1/_2$ fl oz) orange juice

$^1/_2$ cup (125 ml/4 fl oz) vegetable stock

1 Drain the tofu, then slice each block into six lengthways. Place in a single layer in a flat non-metallic dish. Mix the juice, sugar, soy sauce, coriander, garlic and ginger in a jug, then pour over the tofu. Cover and refrigerate overnight, turning once.

2 Drain the tofu, reserving the marinade. Heat the oil in a large frying pan and cook the tofu in batches over high heat for 2–3 minutes each side, or until golden. Remove and keep warm. Bring the marinade to the boil in a saucepan, then reduce the heat and simmer for 1 minute. Remove from the heat and keep warm.

3 Heat a wok, add the bok choy and 1 tablespoon water and cook, covered, over medium heat for 2–3 minutes, or until tender. Remove and keep warm.

4 Put all the sauce ingredients in a saucepan, bring to the boil, then reduce the heat and simmer, covered, for 5–6 minutes, or until the carrot is tender. Transfer to a food processor and blend until smooth.

5 To serve, divide the bok choy among six plates. Top with some sauce, then the tofu and drizzle on a little of the marinade before serving.

TOFU WITH CARROT AND GINGER SAUCE

INGREDIENTS

400 g (14 oz) orecchiette, or conchiglie or cavatelli
450 g (1 lb) Roma (plum) tomatoes
310 g (1¼ cups) ricotta cheese
40 g (1½ oz) Parmesan cheese, grated, plus extra, to serve
8 basil leaves, torn into pieces

1   Cook the pasta in a large saucepan of boiling salted water until al dente.

2   Score a cross in the top of each tomato, plunge them into boiling water (you can use the pasta water) for 20 seconds, then drain and peel the skin away from the cross. Core and chop the tomatoes. Mash the ricotta, then add the Parmesan and season with salt and freshly ground black pepper.

3   Drain the pasta and return to the pan. Add the ricotta mixture, the tomato and basil. Season and toss. Serve at once with Parmesan.

INGREDIENTS

500 g (1 lb 2 oz) toor dal (yellow lentils)
5 pieces of kokum, each 5 cm (2 inch) long (see note)
2 teaspoons coriander (cilantro) seeds
2 teaspoons cumin seeds
2 tablespoons oil
2 teaspoons black mustard seeds
10 curry leaves
7 cloves
10 cm (4 inch) piece of cinnamon stick
5 green chillies, finely chopped
$^1\!/_2$ teaspoon ground turmeric
400 g (14 oz) can chopped tomatoes
20 g ($^3\!/_4$ oz) jaggery or soft brown sugar, or 10 g ($^1\!/_4$ oz) molasses
coriander (cilantro) leaves

1 Soak the lentils in cold water for 2 hours. Rinse the kokum, remove any stones and put in a bowl with cold water for a few minutes to soften. Drain the lentils and place in a heavy-based pan with 1 litre (4 cups) water and the kokum. Bring slowly to the boil, then simmer for 40 minutes, or until the lentils feel soft when pressed.

2 Place a small frying pan over low heat and dry-roast the coriander seeds until aromatic. Remove and dry-roast the cumin seeds. Grind the roasted seeds to a fine powder using a spice grinder or mortar and pestle.

3 Heat the oil in a small pan over low heat. Add the mustard seeds and allow to pop. Add the curry leaves, cloves, cinnamon, chilli, turmeric and the roasted spice mix and cook for 1 minute. Add the tomato and cook for 2–3 minutes, or until the tomato is soft and can be broken up easily. Add the jaggery, then pour the spicy mixture into the simmering lentils and cook for 10 minutes. Season with salt. Garnish with coriander leaves.

NOTE Kokum is the sticky dried purple fruit of the gamboge tree. It imparts an acid fruity flavour to Indian cuisine. Sold in Indian food shops.

INGREDIENTS

$1/4$ cup (60 ml) olive oil
1 large red capsicum (pepper), seeded and cut into quarters
1 large eggplant (aubergine), sliced into 1 cm rounds, then in half again
400 g can chopped tomatoes
1 tablespoon harissa paste (see note)
1 tablespoon Moroccan spice blend
1 cup (250 ml) vegetable stock
2 large zucchini (courgette), cut into 2 cm chunks
$1^1/2$ cups (225 g) couscous
20 g butter

1 Heat 1 tablespoon of the oil in a saucepan over medium–high heat. Sauté the capsicum, skin-side-down, covered, for 3–4 minutes, or until the skin is well browned. Remove from the pan. Peel, then cut the flesh into 1 cm slices. Heat the remaining oil in the pan and cook the eggplant in batches over medium–high heat for 4–5 minutes, or until well browned.

2 Return the capsicum to the pan, then stir in the tomato, harissa paste and Moroccan spice blend. Pour in the stock and bring to the boil. Reduce the heat to medium–low and simmer, uncovered, for 15 minutes. Add the zucchini and eggplant and cook for another 8 minutes, or until the vegetables are tender.

3 About 10 minutes before the vegetables are ready, place the couscous in a heatproof bowl, add $1^1/2$ cups (375 ml) boiling water, and leave for 3–5 minutes. Stir in the butter and fluff with a fork until the butter has melted and the grains separate. Serve the vegetable tagine with the couscous.

NOTE Harissa is a blend of chillies, garlic, spices and oil available at specialist food stores.

INGREDIENTS

200 g (1 cup) dried haricot beans
$^1/_4$ teaspoon saffron threads
2 tablespoons olive oil
1 onion, diced
1 red capsicum (pepper), cut into 1 x 4 cm ($^1/_2$ x $1^1/_2$ inch) strips
5 garlic cloves, crushed
275 g ($1^1/_4$ cups) paella or arborio rice
1 tablespoon sweet paprika
$^1/_2$ teaspoon mixed spice
750 ml (3 cups) vegetable stock
400 g (14 oz) can chopped tomatoes
$1^1/_2$ tablespoons tomato paste (purée)
150 g ($5^1/_2$ oz) fresh or frozen soya beans (see note)
100 g ($3^1/_2$ oz) silverbeet (Swiss chard) leaves (no stems), shredded
400 g (14 oz) can artichoke hearts, drained and quartered
4 tablespoons chopped coriander (cilantro) leaves

1   Put the haricot beans in a bowl, cover with cold water and soak overnight. Drain and rinse well. Place the saffron threads in a small frying pan over medium–low heat. Dry-fry, shaking the pan, for 1 minute, or until darkened. Remove from the heat and, when cool, crumble into a small bowl. Pour in 125 ml ($^1/_2$ cup) warm water and allow to steep.

2   Heat the oil in a large paella or frying pan. Add the onion and capsicum and cook over medium–high heat for 4–5 minutes, or until the onion is soft. Stir in the garlic and cook for 1 minute. Reduce the heat and add the beans, rice, paprika, mixed spice and $^1/_2$ teaspoon salt. Stir to coat. Add the saffron water, stock, tomato and tomato paste and bring to the boil. Cover, reduce the heat and simmer for 20 minutes.

3   Stir in the soya beans, silverbeet and artichoke hearts and cook, covered, for 8 minutes, or until all the liquid is absorbed and the rice and beans are tender. Turn off the heat and leave for 5 minutes. Stir in the coriander just before serving.

NOTE   Fresh or frozen soya beans are available from Asian grocery stores.

VEGETARIAN PAELLA

BAKED MACARONI WITH BUTTER SAUCE

INGREDIENTS

200 g (6¹/₂ oz) macaroni
150 g (5 oz) butter
¹/₄ cup (30 g/1 oz) plain (all-purpose) flour
2¹/₂ cups (600 ml/20 fl oz) milk
1 egg, lightly beaten
1¹/₂ cups (185 g/6 oz) grated Cheddar
2 cloves garlic, crushed
2 ripe tomatoes, seeded and diced

1 Preheat the oven to moderate 180°C (350°F/Gas 4). Lightly grease four shallow 1-cup (250 ml/8 fl oz) ovenproof dishes. Cook the pasta in a large pan of rapidly boiling salted water until al dente. Drain well and return to the pan to keep warm. Meanwhile, melt 60 g (2 oz) of the butter in a large saucepan, add the flour and cook, stirring, over low heat for 1 minute. Remove from the heat and gradually add the milk, stirring until smooth. Return to the heat and cook, stirring, over medium heat for 4 minutes, or until the mixture boils and thickens. Reduce the heat and simmer for 1 minute. Remove from the heat and season well.

2 Add the pasta, egg and two-thirds of the cheese and stir until well combined. Spoon into the dishes and sprinkle with the remaining cheese. Place in a roasting tin and pour enough boiling water into the tin to come halfway up the sides of the dishes. Bake for 25 minutes, or until set. Remove from the roasting tin and leave to rest for 5 minutes.

3 To make the sauce, melt the remaining butter in a frying pan. Add the garlic and tomato and stir over medium heat for 2 minutes. Unmould the baked macaroni onto plates and spoon the warm sauce around the outside. Serve immediately.

INGREDIENTS

1/2 butternut pumpkin (squash) (600 g/1 1/4 lb), peeled and
  seeded

2 tablespoons olive oil

3 teaspoons finely chopped fresh rosemary

1 teaspoon sea salt flakes

1/4 cup (60 ml/2 fl oz) lime juice

1/4 cup (60 ml/2 fl oz) white wine

1/4 cup (60 ml/2 fl oz) vegetable stock

3 French shallots, finely chopped

1 clove garlic, crushed

1/4 teaspoon white pepper

1 tablespoon cream

150 g (5 oz) butter, chilled and cut into small cubes

2 teaspoons finely diced mustard fruit (see note)

100 g (3 1/2 oz) fresh lasagne sheets, cut into eight 8 cm
  (3 inch) squares

100 g (3 1/2 oz) ricotta

1 amaretti cookie, crushed (optional) (see note)

small sprigs fresh rosemary, to garnish

1. Preheat the oven to moderately hot 200°C (400°F/Gas 6). Cut the piece of pumpkin in half, then each half into eight slices. Place half the oil, 2 teaspoons of the rosemary and the salt in a bowl and toss the pumpkin slices through the mixture.

2. Put the pumpkin in a single layer on a baking tray and bake for 25–30 minutes, or until cooked and slightly caramelised. Remove from the oven, cover and keep warm.

3. Meanwhile, combine the lime juice, wine, stock, shallots, garlic, white pepper and the remaining rosemary in a small saucepan and simmer for about 15–20 minutes, or until the liquid has reduced to about 2 tablespoons. Strain into a small clean saucepan, then add the cream and simmer for 2–3 minutes, or until thickened slightly. Whisk in the butter a few cubes at a time until all the butter is incorporated and the sauce is thickened, smooth and glossy. Remove from the heat and stir in the mustard fruit. Season with salt and pepper and leave covered.

4. Fill a large saucepan with water, add the remaining oil and bring to the boil, then reduce to a simmer. Add the lasagne squares in batches and cook, stirring, for 1–2 minutes, or until al dente. Drain well.

5. Gently reheat the pumpkin and the lime butter if necessary. To assemble, place one lasagne square on each plate. Place two slices of pumpkin onto each square, top with one quarter of the ricotta, then top with another two slices of pumpkin and finish with a final layer of lasagne. Give the lime butter a quick whisk, then spoon a little over the top and around the lasagne on the plate. Season with salt and pepper. Sprinkle the top of each lasagne with a little of the crushed amaretti and some fresh rosemary.

NOTE Mustard fruit is a piquant fruit relish made from crystallised fruits preserved in white wine, honey and mustard. Buy it and amaretti from delicatessens and gourmet food stores.

INGREDIENTS

500 g (1 lb) cotelli
2 cups (300 g/10 oz) frozen peas
2 cups (300 g/10 oz) frozen broad beans
$^1/_3$ cup (80 ml/2$^3/_4$ fl oz) olive oil
6 spring onions, cut into short pieces
2 cloves garlic, finely chopped
1 cup (250 ml/8 fl oz) chicken stock
12 asparagus spears, chopped
1 lemon

1   Cook the pasta in a large pan of rapidly boiling salted water until al dente. Drain and return to the pan to keep warm.

2   Meanwhile, cook the peas in a saucepan of boiling water for 1–2 minutes, or until tender. Remove with a slotted spoon and plunge into cold water. Add the broad beans to the same saucepan of boiling water and cook for 1–2 minutes, then drain and plunge into cold water. Remove and slip out of their skins.

3   Heat 2 tablespoons of the oil in a frying pan. Add the spring onion and garlic and cook over medium heat for 2 minutes, or until softened. Pour in the stock and cook for 5 minutes, or until slightly reduced. Add the asparagus and cook for 3–4 minutes, or until bright green and just tender. Stir in the peas and broad beans and cook for 2–3 minutes to heat through.

4   Toss the remaining oil through the pasta, then add the vegetable mixture, $^1/_2$ teaspoon finely grated lemon rind and $^1/_4$ cup (60 ml/2 fl oz) lemon juice. Season and toss together well. Serve with Parmesan shavings.

INGREDIENTS

300 g (10 oz) plain (all-purpose) flour
3 eggs, beaten
3 tablespoons oil
1 cup (250 g/8 oz) ricotta
2 tablespoons grated Parmesan
2 teaspoons chopped chives
1 tablespoon chopped fresh flat-leaf parsley
2 teaspoons chopped fresh basil
1 teaspoon chopped fresh lemon thyme or thyme
1 egg, beaten, extra

1   Sift the flour into a bowl and make a well in the centre. Gradually mix in the eggs and oil. Turn out onto a lightly floured surface and knead for 6 minutes, or until smooth. Cover with plastic wrap and leave for 30 minutes.

2   To make the filling, mix the ricotta, Parmesan and herbs. Season well.

3   Divide the dough into four portions and shape each into a log. Keeping the unworked portions covered, take one portion and flatten it with one or two rolls of a rolling pin. With machine rollers set to the widest setting, crank the dough through two or three times. Fold it into thirds, turn the dough by 90 degrees and feed it through again. If the dough feels sticky, flour it lightly each time it is rolled. Repeat the rolling and folding 8–10 times until the dough feels smooth and elastic. Reduce the width of the rollers by one setting and pass the dough through without folding it. Repeat, setting the rollers one notch closer each time until you have reached a thickness of 2 mm ($\frac{1}{6}$ inch). Roll another sheet slightly larger than the first and cover with a tea towel.

4   Spread the smaller sheet out onto a work surface. Spoon 1 teaspoon of the filling at 5 cm (2 inch) intervals. Brush the beaten egg between the filling along the cutting lines. Place the larger sheet on top. Press the two sheets together along the cutting line. Cut the ravioli with a pastry wheel or knife. Transfer to a lightly floured baking tray. Repeat with the remaining dough and filling. Can be stored in the refrigerator for 1–2 days.

5   Cook the ravioli in a large pan of rapidly boiling water for 5–8 minutes and top with a sauce of your choice.

PASTA, TOMATO AND ARTICHOKE GRILL

350 g (12 oz) pasta
285 g (9 oz) jar marinated artichoke hearts, drained and chopped
2 tablespoons olive oil
1 cup (250 ml/8 fl oz) thick cream
2 tablespoons chopped fresh thyme
2 cloves garlic, crushed
$^3/_4$ cup (75 g/2$^1/_2$ oz) grated Parmesan
1$^2/_3$ cups (200 g/6$^1/_2$ oz) grated Cheddar
1 kg (2 lb) tomatoes, thinly sliced

1 Cook the pasta in a large pan of rapidly boiling salted water until al dente. Drain well. Grease a 23 x 30 cm (9 x 12 inch) ovenproof dish. Stir the artichokes, olive oil, cream, thyme, garlic, half the Parmesan and 1$^1/_4$ cups (150 g/5 oz) of the Cheddar through the hot pasta and season well. Spread evenly into the prepared dish.

2 Arrange the tomatoes over the top, overlapping. Season and sprinkle with the remaining Cheddar and Parmesan. Grill for 6 minutes to brown the top.

650 g (1 lb 5 oz) pumpkin
2 tablespoons olive oil
500 g (1 lb) ricotta
$^1/_3$ cup (60 g/2 oz) pine nuts, toasted
$^3/_4$ cup (35 g/1 oz) fresh basil
2 cloves garlic, crushed
$^1/_3$ cup (30 g/1 oz) grated Parmesan
125 g (4 oz) fresh lasagne sheets
$1^1/_4$ cups (185 g/6 oz) grated mozzarella

1 Preheat the oven to moderate 180°C (350°F/Gas 4). Lightly grease a baking tray. Cut the pumpkin into thin slices and arrange in a single layer on the tray. Brush with oil and cook for 1 hour, or until softened, turning halfway through cooking.

2 Mix together the ricotta, pine nuts, basil, garlic and Parmesan.

3 Brush a square 20 cm (8 inch) ovenproof dish with oil. Cook the pasta according to the packet instructions. Arrange one-third of the pasta sheets over the base of the dish. Spread with the ricotta mixture. Top with half the remaining lasagne sheets.

4 Arrange the pumpkin evenly over the pasta with as few gaps as possible. Season with salt and cracked black pepper and top with the final layer of pasta sheets. Sprinkle with mozzarella. Bake for 20–25 minutes, or until the cheese is golden. Leave for 10 minutes, then cut into squares.

NOTE If the pasta has no cooking instructions, blanch the sheets one at a time.

PUMPKIN, BASIL AND RICOTTA LASAGNE

INGREDIENTS

1.5 kg (3 lb) butternut pumpkin (squash), cut into small cubes
4 cloves garlic, crushed
3 teaspoons fresh thyme leaves
100 ml (3$^1/_2$ fl oz) olive oil
500 g (1 lb) pappardelle
2 tablespoons cream
$^3/_4$ cup (185 ml/6 fl oz) hot chicken stock
30 g (1 oz) shaved Parmesan

1 Preheat the oven to moderately hot 200°C (400°F/Gas 6). Place the pumpkin, garlic, thyme and $^1/_4$ cup (60 ml/2 fl oz) of the olive oil in a bowl and toss together. Season with salt, transfer to a baking tray and cook for 30 minutes, or until tender and golden. Meanwhile, cook the pasta in a large pan of rapidly boiling salted water until al dente. Drain and return to the pan. Toss through the remaining oil and keep warm.

2 Place the pumpkin and cream in a food processor or blender and process until smooth. Add the hot stock and process until smooth. Season with salt and cracked black pepper and gently toss through the pasta. Serve with Parmesan and extra thyme leaves.

INGREDIENTS

2 orange sweet potatoes (about 800 g/1 lb 10 oz in total)
½ cup (90 g/3 oz) ditalini
30 g (1 oz) toasted pine nuts
2 cloves garlic, crushed
4 tablespoons finely chopped fresh basil
½ cup (50 g/1¾ oz) grated Parmesan
⅓ cup (35 g/1¼ oz) dry breadcrumbs
plain (all-purpose) flour, for dusting
olive oil, for shallow-frying

1   Preheat the oven to very hot 250°C (500°F/Gas 10). Pierce the sweet potatoes several times with a fork, then place in a roasting tin and roast for about 1 hour, or until soft. Remove from the oven and cool. Meanwhile, cook the pasta in a large saucepan of boiling water until al dente. Drain and rinse under running water.

2   Peel the sweet potato and mash the flesh with a potato masher or fork, then add the pine nuts, garlic, basil, Parmesan, breadcrumbs and the pasta and combine. Season.

3   Shape the mixture into eight even patties (about 1.5 cm/⅝ inch thick) with floured hands, then lightly dust the patties with flour. Heat the oil in a large frying pan and cook the patties in batches over medium heat for 2 minutes each side, or until golden and heated through. Drain on crumpled paper towels, sprinkle with salt and serve immediately. Great with a fresh green salad.

NOTE   To save time, drop spoonfuls of the mixture into the pan and flatten with an oiled spatula.

INGREDIENTS

200 g (6½ oz) risoni
40 g (1¼ oz) butter
4 spring onions, thinly sliced
400 g (13 oz) zucchini (courgette), grated
4 eggs
1/2 cup (125 ml/4 fl oz) cream
100 g (3½ oz) ricotta (see note)
⅔ cup (100 g/3½ oz) grated mozzarella
¾ cup (75 g/2½ oz) grated Parmesan

1 Preheat the oven to moderate 180°C (350°F/Gas 4). Cook the pasta in a large saucepan of boiling water until al dente. Drain well. Meanwhile, heat the butter in a frying pan, add the spring onion and cook for 1 minute, then add the zucchini and cook for a further 4 minutes, or until soft. Cool slightly.

2 Place the eggs, cream, ricotta, mozzarella, risoni and half of the Parmesan in a bowl and mix together well. Stir in the zucchini mixture, then season with salt and pepper. Spoon the mixture into four 2 cup (500 ml/16 fl oz) greased ovenproof dishes, but do not fill to the brim. Sprinkle with the remaining Parmesan and cook for 25–30 minutes, or until firm and golden.

NOTE With such simple flavours, it is important to use good-quality fresh ricotta from the delicatessen or the deli section of your local supermarket.

Pizza base

7 g ($^1/_4$ oz) sachet dry yeast

$^3/_4$ cup (90 g/3 oz) plain (all-purpose) flour

$^3/_4$ cup (110 g/3$^1/_2$ oz) wholemeal plain (all-purpose) flour

1 tablespoon olive oil

1 tablespoon oil

2 onions, sliced

2 teaspoons soft brown sugar

1–2 tablespoons olive paste

250 g (8 oz) cherry tomatoes, halved

200 g (6$^1/_2$ oz) feta cheese, crumbled

3 tablespoons shredded fresh basil

1 To make the dough, mix the yeast and flours in a large bowl. Make a well in the centre and add the olive oil and $^1/_2$ cup (125 ml/4 fl oz) warm water. Mix well, adding a little more water if necessary, then gather together with your hands. Turn out and knead on a lightly floured surface for 5 minutes. Place in a lightly oiled bowl, cover with plastic wrap and leave in a draught-free place for 1 hour.

2 Meanwhile, heat the oil in a frying pan and cook the onion over medium–low heat for 20 minutes, stirring regularly. Add the sugar and cook, stirring, for 1–2 minutes, or until caramelized. Set aside to cool.

3 Preheat the oven to hot 220°C (425°F/Gas 7). Punch down the dough and knead for 1 minute. Roll out to a 30 cm (12 inches) round (it will shrink as you roll it), then tuck the edge of the dough under to create a rim. Sprinkle an oven tray lightly with polenta or brush with oil, and place the dough on the tray.

4 Spread the paste over the dough, leaving a narrow border, then top with the onion. Arrange the tomato halves over the onion, and sprinkle with feta and basil. Bake for 25 minutes.

FETA, TOMATO AND OLIVE PIZZA

INGREDIENTS

Pastry
1 cup (125 g/4 oz) plain (all-purpose) flour
60 g (2 oz) chilled butter, chopped
1 egg yolk
2 teaspoons poppy seeds
1–2 tablespoons iced water

30 g (1 oz) butter
2 tablespoons oil
1 onion, cut into thin wedges
1 leek, sliced
3 potatoes, cut into large chunks
300 g (10 oz) orange sweet potato (kumera), cut into large chunks
300 g (10 oz) pumpkin, cut into large chunks
200 g (6^1/$_2$ oz) swede, peeled and cut into large chunks
1 cup (250 ml/8 fl oz) vegetable stock
1 red capsicum (pepper), cut into large pieces
200 g (6^1/$_2$ oz) broccoli, cut into large florets
2 zucchini (courgette), cut into large pieces
1 cup (125 g/4 oz) grated vintage Cheddar

1   Preheat the oven to moderately hot 200°C (400°F/Gas 6). To make the pastry, sift the flour into a large bowl and add the butter. Rub the butter in with your fingertips until it resembles fine breadcrumbs. Make a well in the centre and add the egg yolk, poppy seeds and water and mix with a flat-bladed knife, using a cutting action, until the mixture comes together in beads. Gently gather the dough together and lift out onto a lightly floured work surface. Press the dough together into a ball and flatten it slightly into a disc, wrap in plastic wrap and refrigerate for 20 minutes.

2   Roll the dough out between two sheets of baking paper, then remove the top sheet and invert the pastry over a 23 cm (9 inch) pie plate. Use a small ball of pastry to help press the pastry into the plate then trim the edge. Prick the base with a fork and bake for 15–20 minutes, or until dry to the touch and golden.

3   To make the filling, heat the butter and oil in a large saucepan, add the onion and leek and cook over medium heat for 5 minutes, or until soft and golden. Add the potato, sweet potato, pumpkin and swede and cook, stirring occasionally, until the vegetables start to soften. Add the stock and simmer for 30 minutes.

4   Add the remaining vegetables, reduce the heat and simmer for 20 minutes, or until the vegetables are soft—some may break up slightly. The mixture should be just mushy. Season to taste with salt and pepper. Allow the mixture to cool a little.

5   Spoon the mixture into the shell, sprinkle with cheese and cook under a medium grill for 5–10 minutes, or until the cheese is golden brown.

INGREDIENTS

7 g (¼ oz) sachet dry yeast
1 teaspoon sugar
2 tablespoons olive oil
2½ cups (310 g/10 oz) plain (all-purpose) flour, sifted

Pizza Topping
1 tablespoon tomato paste (purée)
1 large red capsicum (pepper), thinly sliced
125 g (4 oz) marinated artichoke hearts, quartered
¼ cup (30 g/1 oz) black olives, pitted
200 g (6½ oz) bocconcini, thickly sliced

1 Combine the yeast, ¾ cup (185 ml/6 fl oz) of warm water and the sugar in a bowl and set aside in a warm place for 5–10 minutes, or until frothy. Put the oil, flour and 1 teaspoon salt in a large bowl, add the frothy yeast and mix to a soft dough.

2 Turn the dough out onto a lightly floured surface and knead for 10 minutes, or until smooth and elastic. Roll into a ball and place in a large oiled bowl. Cover with oiled plastic wrap and set aside in a warm place for 1 hour, or until the dough has doubled in size.

3 Preheat the oven to moderate 180°C (350°F/Gas 4). Punch down the dough with your fist to expel any air, and knead for 1 minute. Roll into a flat disc large enough to fit into a greased 23 cm (9 inch) springform tin. Press into the tin, cover with a tea towel and leave to rise for about 20 minutes.

4 Spread the tomato paste over the dough and arrange the other topping ingredients, except for the bocconcini, on top. Bake for 20 minutes, remove from the oven and spread the slices of bocconcini over the top, then bake for a further 20 minutes, or until the dough is well risen and firm to the touch in the centre. Cool on a wire rack before cutting and serving.

INGREDIENTS

2 slender eggplants (aubergines), halved and cut into thick slices
350 g (11 oz) pumpkin, chopped
2 zucchini (courgettes), halved and cut into thick slices
1–2 tablespoons olive oil
1 large red capsicum (pepper), chopped
1 teaspoon olive oil, extra
1 red onion, cut into thin wedges
1 tablespoon Korma curry paste
plain yoghurt, to serve

Pastry
1½ cups (185 g/6 oz) plain (all-purpose) flour
125 g (4 oz) butter, chopped
⅔ cup (100 g/3½ oz) roasted cashews, finely chopped
1 teaspoon cumin seeds
2–3 tablespoons chilled water

1 Preheat the oven to moderately hot 200°C (400°F/Gas 6). Put the eggplant, pumpkin and zucchini on a lined oven tray, then brush with oil and bake for 30 minutes. Turn, add the capsicum and bake for 30 minutes. Cool.

2 Meanwhile, heat the extra oil in a frying pan and cook the onion for 2–3 minutes, or until soft. Add the curry paste and cook, stirring, for 1 minute, or until fragrant and well mixed. Cool. Reduce the oven to moderate 180°C (350°F/Gas 4).

3 To make the pastry, sift the flour into a large bowl and add the butter. Rub the butter into the flour with your fingertips until it resembles fine breadcrumbs. Stir in the cashews and cumin seeds. Make a well in the centre and add the water. Mix with a flat-bladed knife, using a cutting action, until the mixture comes together in beads. Gather the dough together and lift out onto a sheet of baking paper. Flatten to a disc, then roll out to a 35 cm (14 inch) circle.

4 Lift onto an oven tray and spread the onion mixture over the pastry, leaving a wide border. Arrange the other vegetables over the onion, piling them slightly higher in the centre. Working your way around, fold the edge of the pastry in pleats over the vegetables. Bake for 45 minutes, or until the pastry is golden. Serve immediately with plain yoghurt.

INGREDIENTS

Pastry
2 cups (250 g/8 oz) plain (all-purpose) flour
30 g (1 oz) chilled butter, chopped
¼ cup (60 ml) olive oil

Filling
500 g (1 lb) English spinach leaves
2 teaspoons olive oil
1 onion, finely chopped
3 spring onions, finely chopped
200 g (6½ oz) feta, crumbled
2 tablespoons chopped fresh flat-leaf parsley
1 tablespoon chopped fresh dill
2 tablespoons grated kefalotyri cheese
¼ cup (45 g/1½ oz) cooked white rice
¼ cup (40 g/1½ oz) pine nuts, toasted and roughly chopped
¼ teaspoon ground nutmeg
½ teaspoon ground cumin
3 eggs, lightly beaten

1   Lightly grease a shallow 17 x 26 cm (7 x 10 inch) tin. To make the pastry, sift the flour and ½ teaspoon salt into a large bowl. Rub in the butter until it resembles fine breadcrumbs. Make a well in the centre and add the oil. Using your hands, mix together. Add ½ cup (125 ml/4 fl oz) warm water and mix with a flat-bladed knife, in a cutting action, until the mixture comes together in beads. Gently gather the dough together and lift out onto a lightly floured surface. Press into a ball and flatten into a disc. Wrap in plastic wrap and refrigerate for 1 hour.

2   Trim and wash the spinach, then coarsely chop the leaves and stems. Wrap in a tea towel and squeeze out as much moisture as possible. Heat the oil in a frying pan, add the onion and spring onion and cook over low heat, without browning, for 5 minutes, or until softened. Place in a bowl with the spinach and the remaining filling ingredients and mix well. Season.

3   Preheat the oven to moderately hot 200°C (400°F/Gas 6). Roll out just over half the pastry between two sheets of baking paper, remove the top sheet and invert the pastry into the tin. Use a small ball of pastry to help press the pastry into the tin, allowing any excess to hang over the sides. Spoon the filling into the tin. Roll out the remaining pastry until large enough to cover the top. Place over the filling and press the two pastry edges firmly together to seal. Use a small sharp knife to trim away any extra pastry. Brush the top with a little oil, then score three strips lengthways, then on the diagonal to make a diamond pattern on the surface. Make two slits in the top to allow steam to escape.

4   Bake for 45–50 minutes, covering with foil if the surface becomes too brown. The pie is cooked when it slides when the tin is gently shaken. Turn out onto a rack for 10 minutes, then cut into pieces and serve.

INGREDIENTS

2 tablespoons olive oil

1 large leek, finely chopped

2 cloves garlic, crushed

125 g (4 oz) button mushrooms, roughly chopped

2 teaspoons ground cumin

2 teaspoons ground coriander (cilantro)

½ cup (95 g/3 oz) brown or green lentils

½ cup (125 g/4 oz) red lentils

2 cups (500 ml/16 fl oz) vegetable stock

300 g (10 oz) sweet potato, diced

4 tablespoons finely chopped fresh coriander (cilantro) leaves

8 sheets ready-rolled puff pastry

1 egg, lightly beaten

½ leek, extra, cut into thin strips

200 g (6½ oz) plain yoghurt

2 tablespoons grated Lebanese cucumber

½ teaspoon soft brown sugar

1   Preheat the oven to moderately hot 200°C (400°F/Gas 6). Heat the oil in a saucepan over medium heat and cook the leek for 2–3 minutes, or until soft. Add the garlic, mushrooms, cumin and ground coriander and cook for 1 minute, or until fragrant.

2   Add the combined lentils and stock and bring to the boil. Reduce the heat and simmer for 20–25 minutes, or until the lentils are cooked through, stirring occasionally. Add the sweet potato in the last 5 minutes.

3   Transfer to a bowl and stir in the coriander. Season to taste. Cool.

4   Cut the pastry sheets into four even squares. Place 1½ tablespoons of filling into the centre of each square and bring the edges together to form a pouch. Pinch together, then tie each pouch with string. Lightly brush with egg and place on lined baking trays. Bake for 20–25 minutes, or until the pastry is puffed and golden.

5   Soak the leek strips in boiling water for 30 seconds. Remove the string and re-tie with a piece of blanched leek. Put the yoghurt, cucumber and sugar in a bowl and mix together well. Serve with the pastry pouches.

INGREDIENTS

1¾ cups (215 g/7 oz) plain (all-purpose) flour

120 g (4 oz) chilled butter, cubed

¼ cup (60 ml/2 fl oz) cream

1–2 tablespoons chilled water

1 large (250 g/8 oz) Desiree potato, cut into 2 cm (1 inch) cubes

1 tablespoon olive oil

2 cloves garlic, crushed

1 red capsicum (pepper), cut into cubes

1 red onion, sliced into rings

2 zucchini (courgettes), sliced

2 tablespoons chopped fresh dill

1 tablespoon chopped fresh thyme

1 tablespoon drained baby capers

150 g (5 oz) marinated quartered artichoke hearts, drained

⅔ cup (30 g/1 oz) baby English spinach leaves

Salsa verde

1 clove garlic

2 cups (40 g/1¼ oz) fresh flat-leaf parsley

⅓ cup (80 ml/2¾ fl oz) extra virgin olive oil

3 tablespoons chopped fresh dill

1½ tablespoons Dijon mustard

1 tablespoon red wine vinegar

1 tablespoon drained baby capers

1 Sift the flour and ½ teaspoon salt into a large bowl. Add the butter and rub it into the flour with your fingertips until it resembles fine breadcrumbs. Add the cream and water and mix with a flat-bladed knife until the mixture comes together in beads. Gather together and lift onto a lightly floured work surface. Press into a ball, then flatten into a disc, wrap in plastic wrap and refrigerate for 30 minutes.

2 Preheat the oven to moderately hot 200°C (400°F/Gas 6). Grease a 27 cm (11 inch) loose-bottomed flan tin. Roll the dough out between two sheets of baking paper large enough to line the tin. Remove the paper and invert the pastry into the tin. Use a small pastry ball to press the pastry into the tin, allowing any excess to hang over the side. Roll a rolling pin over the tin, cutting off any excess. Cover the pastry with a piece of crumpled baking paper, then add baking beads. Place the tin on a baking tray and bake for 15–20 minutes. Remove the paper and beads, reduce the heat to moderate 180°C (350°F/Gas 4) and bake for 20 minutes, or until golden.

3 To make the salsa verde, combine all the ingredients in a food processor and process until almost smooth.

4 Boil the potato until just tender. Drain. Heat the oil in a large frying pan and cook the garlic, capsicum and onion over medium heat for 3 minutes, stirring frequently. Add the zucchini, dill, thyme and capers and cook for 3 minutes. Reduce the heat to low, add the potato and artichokes, and heat through. Season to taste.

5 To assemble, spread 3 tablespoons of the salsa over the pastry. Spoon the vegetable mixture into the case and drizzle with half the remaining salsa. Pile the spinach in the centre and drizzle with the remaining salsa.

All our recipes are thoroughly tested in a specially developed test kitchen. Standard metric measuring cups and spoons are used in the development of our recipes. All cup and spoon measurements are level. We have used 60 g (2¼ oz/Grade 3) eggs in all recipes. Sizes of cans vary from manufacturer to manufacturer and between countries – use the can size closest to the one suggested in the recipe.

CONVERSION GUIDE

1 cup = 250 ml (9 fl oz)	1 Australian tablespoon = 20 ml (4 teaspoons)
1 teaspoon = 5 ml	1 UK/US tablespoon = 15 ml (3 teaspoons)

DRY MEASURES
30 g = 1 oz
250 g = 9 oz
500 g = 1 lb 2 oz

LIQUID MEASURES
30 ml = 1 fl oz
125 ml = 4 fl oz
250 ml = 9 fl oz

LINEAR MEASURES
6 mm = ¼ inch
1 cm = ½ inch
2.5 cm = 1 inch

CUP CONVERSIONS – DRY INGREDIENTS
1 cup almonds, slivered whole = 125 g (4½ oz)
1 cup cheese, lightly packed processed cheddar = 155 g (5½ oz)
1 cup wheat flour = 125 g (4½ oz)
1 cup wholemeal flour = 140 g (5 oz)
1 cup minced (ground) meat = 250 g (9 oz)
1 cup pasta shapes = 125 g (4½ oz)
1 cup raisins = 170 g (6 oz)
1 cup rice, short grain, raw = 200 g (7 oz)
1 cup sesame seeds = 160 g (6 oz)
1 cup split peas = 250 g (9 oz)

INTERNATIONAL GLOSSARY
capsicum	sweet bell pepper
chick pea	garbanzo bean
chilli	chile, chili pepper
cornflour	cornstarch
eggplant	aubergine
spring onion	scallion
zucchini	courgette
plain flour	all-purpose flour
prawns	shrimp
minced meat	ground meat

Where temperature ranges are indicated, the lower figure applies to gas ovens, the higher to electric ovens. This allows for the fact that the flame in gas ovens generates a drier heat, which effectively cooks food faster than the moister heat of an electric oven, even if the temperature setting is the same.

	°C	°F	GAS MARK
Very slow	120	250	½
Slow	150	300	2
Mod slow	160	325	3
Moderate	180	350	4
Mod hot	190(g)–210(e)	375–425	5
Hot	200(g)–240(e)	400–475	6
Very hot	230(g)–260(e)	450–525	8

Published in 2006 by Bay Books,
an imprint of Murdoch Books Pty Limited.

ISBN 1-74045-944-X
978-1-74045-944-0

Printed by Sing Cheong Printing Company Ltd.
Printed in China.